CAMPESE

James Curran is Professor of Modern History at
Sydney University. The author of a number
of books on Australian politics and foreign
policy, he is a foreign affairs columnist for the
Australian Financial Review and is writing a
history of Australia–China relations. His poetry
has been published in *Meanjin* and *Quadrant*,
and his rugby writing in *Midi-Olympique*. Curran
played rugby as a five-eighth in the lower grades of
the Sydney club competition in the early 1990s.

CAMPESE

THE LAST OF THE DREAM SELLERS

JAMES CURRAN

SCRIBE

Melbourne • London

Scribe Publications
2 John St, Clerkenwell, London, WC1N 2ES, United Kingdom
18–20 Edward St, Brunswick, Victoria 3056, Australia
3754 Pleasant Ave, Suite 100, Minneapolis, Minnesota 55409, USA

Published by Scribe 2021

Front-cover image: Campese heading for the try line in a World Cup
semi-final in Dublin, 1991.
Back-cover image: The Webb Ellis Cup is held aloft at Twickenham,
November 1991.

Typeset in Adobe Caslon Pro by the publishers

Printed and bound in the UK by CPI Group (UK) Ltd, Croydon
CR0 4YY

Scribe is committed to the sustainable use of natural resources and
the use of paper products made responsibly from those resources.

978 1 914484 09 4 (UK edition)
978 1 922310 57 6 (Australian edition)
978 1 922586 18 6 (ebook)

Catalogue records for this book are available from the National
Library of Australia and the British Library.

scribepublications.co.uk
scribepublications.com.au
scribepublications.com

In loving memory of Bernie Curran
(1945-2021).
My dad, friend, guide, and inspiration.

'Honour to those who in the life they lead
define and guard a Thermopylae'
— CP Cavafy

CONTENTS

FOREWORD

by Bob Dwyer, Wallabies coach 1982–83, 1988–95

'Far better it is to dare mighty things, to win glorious triumphs, even though chequered by failure, than to take rank with those poor spirits who neither enjoy much nor suffer much, because they live in the grey twilight that knows not victory nor defeat.'

It's hard to believe that Theodore Roosevelt was not talking about Campo when he uttered these inspiring words, well over 100 years ago. But he was definitely talking about men of Campo's ilk.

Maybe a half-century later, at the famous Sydney Cricket Ground, a young cricket fan said much the same thing, if a little more succinctly. 'Ave a go, yer mug!' young Stephen Gascogne called out, exhorting an Australian batsman to test his mettle, to stop playing so stodgily safe. We thought so highly of young 'Yabba' and his advice that we now have a bronze statue of him at the SCG. This is more the Aussie way, to exhort the country's champions to dare mighty things. We expect a lot from our heroes and, like Yabba, are not beyond offering advice — even, dare I say it, aggressive criticism!

There is, in some lesser-informed circles at least, a tendency to think of Campo as careless, perhaps even selfish — caring more about his own daring exploits and the acclaim of the crowd than the fate of his own team. Nothing could have been further from the truth.

It is no coincidence that the appearance of a young David Campese in his Wallaby jersey for the first time, in Christchurch, New Zealand, introduced many of the important new ingredients that ultimately took the Wallaby team to world leadership during much of the next two decades.

Further — just the name 'Campo'! If you're known around the world simply by your nickname, you've definitely made it.

I am reminded of the oft-repeated tongue-in-cheek sentence, 'The harder I train, the luckier I get.' Campo was — always — first on the pitch and last off, at every practice session.

He was, undoubtedly, the best-prepared rugby player of his generation — and rewrote the book on what could be achieved, if you put the work in. Strength, agility, speed, acceleration, fitness — all were covered in Campo's regime. As for diet and lifestyle, he shunned anything that could impact negatively on his capacity to be at his best. And, not surprisingly, the better he prepared, the better he performed.

To this day, I remain impressed with the immediate support that Campo had, amongst the (few) more experienced members of his first Wallaby tour squad. This is by no means universal. Frequently, more experienced players are inclined to regard brash newcomers — does this sound accurate? — with extreme suspicion. Not so with Campo's arrival on the scene. As the first test on that 1982 tour drew nearer, I was approached, individually, by more than a couple of the more experienced players on the subject of the impending team selection. 'Pick the young bloke!' was their common advice.

And so, throughout his very long career, Campo continued to win the highest accolades from teammates and opponents from the entire rugby world. (Incidentally, I recently looked up details of his career, in preparation for a lunch in his honour, and confirmed that he is by far our longest-serving Wallaby, with a career spanning fifteen years, followed by (Sir) Nick Shehadie, with eleven years, and daylight third!)

James Curran has, in this book, quoted many of these accolades, and reminded us — and we all need reminding from time to time — of just what a jewel appeared, all those years ago, as if from nowhere, at least to those of us from outside of Queanbeyan, on the rugby pitches in Brisbane and Sydney. From his very first tour in 1982, Campo continued to thrill, even enthral and delight, Aussie sports fans and more than a few non-Aussies too. Teammates welcomed his presence and, I reckon, gained confidence from it. They also knew that his presence caused more than a few doubts in the minds of our opponents — and that perhaps a focus on Campo might give the team opportunities elsewhere.

You will read herein plenty about this in accurate detail from across the world of rugby nations, and from many great players and commentators, of Campo's unparalleled career, but I want to finish this foreword with a focus on what I believe was the most important of his many qualities.

His *courage*!

'No man is an island'. So said John Donne, a few hundred years ago, meaning that each of us exists, not alone, but as a part of a society — and affected and influenced by the opinion of that society, and perhaps, by their acceptance of us as individuals.

Consider then the society to which an individual in the public eye exposes himself and his actions. Consider, further, the size, and the concerns, of the society that watches and examines a major sporting event around the world — often over and over again, and in minute detail.

In the case of a major rugby match, the island is inhabited by hundreds of thousands of people, many with passionate aspirations, and many with firm, though sometimes mistaken, opinions. If you 'make a blue' on this stage — among the spectators, TV and radio broadcasters, slow-motion replays ad infinitum, and newspaper reporters and columnists — you're not going to be allowed to forget it!

Dismiss any suggestion of carelessness or negligence on the part of any player on such a stage. They know the odds and they know the penalties — but they believe implicitly that 'Herein lies success for my team'. Even 'for my country'!

Thank God, then, that providence allows an occasional individual to grace our more mundane lives and expose us to greatness.

Such an individual is David Campese, who, on the world stage, was willing to risk personal failure to achieve success. I have seen Campo distraught — beside himself with grief, even — with the horror that he had 'let everyone down'. Not just his team, but his country.

Still, he managed to call on his undoubted courage and determination to rise again and show us, yet again, just what 'having a go' can do for you — and for the rest of us.

Oh, that we could see his like again!

INTRODUCTION

OFF THE EDGE

In March 1982, moviegoers across the country were treated to one of the more dramatic moments of Australian cinematography. A film that brought to life Banjo Paterson's famous poem 'The Man from Snowy River' raced to its conclusion with a pulsating horse chase through the rugged high country of Victoria, as a crack gathering of stockmen go in search of a prized colt that has escaped and joined a mob of wild bush horses. At the climactic moment of the film, the brumbies disappear by galloping headlong down a mountainside, seemingly out of reach, as if swallowed up by the bush itself. Harrison, a wealthy pastoralist and the colt's owner, can only mutter with a mixture of disdain and resignation that it is time to call it a day. The chase is off.

One rider, however, is not deterred. Launching his 'small and weedy beast' off the summit in hot pursuit, the man from Snowy River careers down the mountain at the most improbable, diabolical angle, cheering as he does so. Even Clancy of the Overflow, played in the film by Jack Thompson, does as Paterson bade him in print, and pulls up short. On screen, Thompson, with eyes squinting, purses his lips in sheer disbelief at the courage unfolding before him. Others watch in awe as the stripling from Snowy River lets 'the pony have his head', racing him down that 'terrible descent' like 'a torrent down its bed'.

These onlookers — so the poem and the film tell us — are rendered passive bystanders, their own bravado puny before the display of bravery that has galloped past them. Indeed, they watch fearfully as the young lad sends 'the flint stones flying' and clears 'the fallen timbers in his stride'. In Australian cinemas, heads are angled, necks craned, and breaths held as Jim Craig — the film deigned to give the legend a name — hurtles off that mountaintop. The soundtrack, itself thundering through a blur of grey gum and eucalypt during the pursuit, suddenly falls silent. A lone trumpet call announces the audacity, but also invites speculation: perhaps the hero's downfall is at hand. Surely no horseman, even one as finely attuned to the local conditions as this, will survive. The end, of course, is otherwise: the man from Snowy River not only makes it down, but succeeds in bringing the mob under control.

For all its location in an older vision of a rustic, Australian bush idyll, there was something particularly apt about an audience in the 1980s being asked to revisit this image of a young, unfancied horseman taking that leap of faith off the summit. Here was a flight into the unknown, an escape.

What attracted readers of so many generations to the poem, and what the film's producers were clearly hoping to reproduce on screen, was its appeal to adventure: its ability, even if only for a short time, to transcend the everyday. As historian Richard White observed of the poem, 'Few of the tens of thousands who would learn it word for word were men of Snowy River, but they all imagined, at that one exhilarating moment of decision at the summit, that they would have sent the flint stones flying too.' At the time of their release in 1895, Paterson's stanzas ennobled the hardy virtues of the Australian bushman, and by extension his readiness for race war and struggle. By the 1980s, however, it had become a story, White notes, of 'individual talent defying convention'.[1]

Only months after the film's release, another slightly built Australian was to strike his own 'firelight ... with every stride' on rugby fields around the country and the world. In August 1982, David Campese, the nineteen-year-old son of an Italian migrant from working-class Queanbeyan, a small town near the nation's capital, put the rugby world on notice in his very first Test match for Australia. Playing in New Zealand at Lancaster Park, Christchurch, and opposite a player widely regarded at the time as the world's finest winger, Stu Wilson, Campese used a combination of raw pace and guile to leave his opponent stranded and, later in the match, to touch down for his first Test try.[2]

Campese had arrived in New Zealand as an unknown quantity, and, much to the displeasure of local punters and pundits, professing ignorance of his more fancied opponent.

'Stu who?' he is reported to have said as he answered reporters' questions about how he felt about facing up to the All Black tyro. Campese, after all, had grown up idolising heroes from Rugby League, especially those who had played in the dominant St George teams of the 1960s, such as Graeme 'Changa' Langlands. In the pen portraits featured in the official program from that Test match, the debutant's occupation was listed as 'saw miller'.[3] There is something almost perfectly, if not deliciously, fitting about that job title, for what Campese did in his day job he was to effectively do to his All Black opponents that afternoon, and later, to teams the world over: slice through gaps and split defences. A rugby correspondent would later write that while few would remember the scores in that series — Australia lost two Tests to one — 'Campese's sparkling running, by contrast, will remain in the memory, a warm glow emanating on cold, dark nights'.[4]

As a rugby player, David Campese did not so much scale the heights of the game as sizzle towards and sometimes beyond its summit. He finished his international career in 1996 holding the world record for the number of tries scored in Test matches, and as the most capped player in Australian rugby history, with 101 to his name. Campese seemed to operate on cross-grained pure instinct: one that left many a defender not only clutching in vain at the invisible, but stranded in his audacity's slipstream. He followed no straight path, observed no rule book. What many players would have liked to pull off once in their careers, Campese seemed to be able to do several times a game. Conjuring wizardry across the open field, his play was unbridled, unstructured, untamed, unpredictable and, at times, uncontrollable. The result was some of the most exhilarating feats ever seen by an Australian sportsman. So the superlatives trailed him for much of his career: hailed as the 'Bradman of rugby' by former Wallaby coach Alan Jones, Campese is widely regarded by the game's most distinguished writers as perhaps the finest player ever to grace a rugby field. Never could it be said of him, either, that he was 'all float and no sting'. As the *Sydney Morning Herald* editorialised on the occasion of his 100th Test, 'for Australians, the allure of Campese is that the running genius he has displayed in the gold jersey has been matched by his effectiveness as a match winner'.[5]

Even if Campese is no longer the household name he was in the 1980s and 1990s, if the expression 'too easy Campese' retains a somewhat tenuous place in the lexicon of the generation who watched him, it is his name, along with that of the Indigenous Ella brothers, which is most closely associated with this era in Australian rugby, when running with the ball was the first instinct of those national teams. When rugby followers today feel nostalgia for a lost golden age, they lament the fading of the free-flowing play of which Campese was the supreme exponent, especially in that period after Mark Ella's retirement from the sport in 1984.

Rugby memories do operate somewhat differently in the Australian sporting imagination: and while there is no doubt Campese has a permanent currency with the game's purists, and some purchase with those who kept half an eye on rugby even as they devoted themselves to Rugby League and Australian Rules, he does not occupy the same niche in the pantheon as a Steve Waugh or Shane Warne. But if it is true, as writer Gideon Haigh suggests, that 'only a tiny sample of feats and personalities endure across generations', the name Campese does just that for rugby and sport in Australia. And it continues to resonate overseas, especially in the United Kingdom, South Africa and New Zealand.[6] Former Wallaby Mark Loane said some years ago that people like Campese 'are getting rarer and rarer in world sports — the player who is prepared to take risks and do something special. Later on, he should be kept in some sort of glass cage for teaching purposes.'[7]

The primary purpose of this book, though, is to take Campese out of that glass cage in an effort to reveal why he so excited those who saw him play. This is a study of his artistry and aesthetic: in short, his creative genius. It is an attempt to understand a player whose sheer individualism upended the conventions associated with rugby — a player who listened to Ravel's *Bolero* before matches, and who, later in his career, would quietly read to himself a poem given to him by his mother prior to each game. Written by the American Nancye Sims, 'Winners Are People Like You' spoke of those who 'fear failing' but 'refuse to let fear control them', and who 'from the ordinary … make the extraordinary'.[8] However difficult it is to describe perfectly his effect on the emotions of those who watched him, and the sheer chutzpah of his devil-take-the-hindmost attitude to playing the game, Campese's expressiveness on the field demands critical appreciation.

While this book is not a biography of Campese, it does seek to understand how a stringy kid from Queanbeyan who left the local high school at the age of sixteen rose to the very top of a sport widely perceived to be the preserve of a privileged private school–educated elite. As it happens, when Campese looked around the dressing room before that first Test in New Zealand back in 1982, nearly half of his teammates came from a working-class background. The gradual disappearance of that demographic from Australian rugby's profile is one important cause of its continuing struggle to remain relevant in today's sporting environment. To this day, Campese feels that the rugby community in Australia never truly embraced him as one of them, and that the sport has since failed to nurture the talent that once flowed so freely from the public education system. Moreover, since the game went professional in the mid-1990s, it has repeatedly squandered the opportunity to genuinely extend its reach and appeal beyond the narrow confines of private schools in Sydney, Canberra, and Brisbane, what the late journalist Wanda Jamrozik once described as 'mock Gothic temples to the cultural cringe'.[9]

Campese would go on to find the popular acceptance he craved elsewhere, especially from adoring crowds in Britain, New Zealand, Italy, and France. And he found that his talent allowed him the opportunity to transcend the boundaries of an amateur sport that, during his career, eventually got dragged, kicking and screaming, into the professional era.

Campese, then, represents in many ways both the great strengths and weaknesses of Australian Rugby Union: the capacity for a player like him to reach its heights, from outside the traditional pathways that fed the elite level of the game, and the inability of the game's administrators to translate that on-field success into a lasting strategy to build rugby's profile.

That, too, may be one reason why the era in which Campese and his teammates won a Grand Slam (in 1984), along with Bledisloe and World Cups (in 1986 and 1991), can appear to be something of a dream. Wallaby supporters can still be found out the back of grandstands today scratching their heads and asking why they had to wake up from it. The subtitle of this book, taken from a newspaper interview with Campese while the Wallabies were touring the south of France in 1993, connected to that dimension of this player, which for so many involved in the game belonged to the imaginary realm. In France, they called him *'le marchand de rêves'*, or 'dream seller'. The profile delivered its verdict via a garland of adjectival laurels, with Campese being labelled as *'incontournable, inégalable, imprévisible, genial, geant, unique, il est tout cela á la fois'* ('unavoidable, unbeatable, unpredictable, a genius, a giant [of the game], unique: he is all of them at once'). David Campese 'was the last star of the rugby world, the most famous player on planet rugby, the last dream seller. Because David Campese makes us dream again.' His play was from 'another planet … that of the magicians. Is he simply an extra-terrestrial? Because it's clear: the Wallabies without Campese are simply not the Wallabies. It's a little like champagne without the bubbles.'[10]

Like so many others whose talents on the field are so rare or special that they defy easy categorisation, Campese's skills were sometimes held to be otherworldly, even inherently history-making. The very fact that so many journalists felt compelled to historicise him even in the midst of his career surely says something about their conviction that he was ushering in something to be remembered — even if his style, as author and writer Malcolm Knox has observed, was not reproduceable.[11] Indeed, it was precisely because his type of play could not be easily copied or mimicked that they sought constantly to capture his contribution, as if to pause it, hold it, before it vanished.

Campese made such an impact that the rugby writers who covered this period were always trying to scale their own rhetorical heights with him, to find a vocabulary, a frame of comparison, to do justice to what was unfolding before them. Alan Jones's comparison of him to Bradman might have grabbed the most headlines — in a way that no other comparison in Australian sport could — but over the course of his career, Campese was to be put on the same level as boxer Muhammad Ali, artist Jackson Pollock, Russian ballet dancer Vaslav Nijinksy, and the Cavaliers of the English Civil War. As rugby writer Spiro Zavos opined, the Cavaliers believed in triumphs that were to 'be achieved by (and with) flair and dash'. Another referred to Campese's 'Mona Lisa' smile — the 'fleeting one which crosses his face after he has scored'.[12]

If it wasn't history being appealed to, mysticism would do. Campese's ability to inspire — to surprise and shock — prompted some to ascribe otherworldly powers to him. At the end of the Rugby World Cup in 1991, for example, the host broadcaster, ITV, made a documentary covering Campese's effect on and contribution to that competition — he was, after all, its top try scorer and the player of the tournament. At its conclusion, the British compere looked skyward to convey Campese's influence on the game: 'David Campese is a world star, a bright and gleaming star in rugby's milky way. With tart contempt, he dismisses the ordinary and refuses to be bound by convention ... to see him in action you witness the sweeter ethic of rugby.'[13] The London *Sunday Times'* noted rugby critic Stephen Jones finished off a column on Campese with a similar cosmic plea: 'Whichever planet you come from, Campo, I wish I could watch rugby there all the time.'[14]

When Campese was named one of the Rothmans international players of the year — rugby's equivalent to the prestigious *Wisden* cricketers of the year — following his efforts in that World Cup, the famous Welsh rugby player Barry John said of him:

> [L]ike Pele, he is associated with the very best and historic moments in sport; he has special genius which shows that an individual can still paint his own portrait and leave an indelible mark for all to treasure. The ingredients are the same: stature, presence, personality, style and an immense belief in the God-given talents.[15]

Campese clearly seems to have been given something of a niche, too, in an age when the achievement of a state of grace in sport — athletic beauty — was associated with the effortless but deadly approach to the wicket of West Indian fast bowler Michael Holding, or the classical form of American sprinter Carl Lewis at the 1984 Olympics, or basketballer Michael Jordan airborne. Campese came to epitomise something of that kind of quality for rugby. Even those proclaiming their own unfamiliarity with the bizarre arcanery of rugby's rules found his attractiveness in play irresistible. Thus, in August 1993, Wanda Jamrozik, who had no prior experience either watching or reporting rugby, wrote that while Campese seemed 'inconsequential' or 'preoccupied' for much of the time he was on the field, it was only ever a misleading prelude to the main event:

> The explosion, when it comes, almost always comes out of nowhere. You don't see the build-up, the positioning, the acceleration. What you see, suddenly, is that Campese is there and that the field is breaking open before your eyes. Where there were crowds of players there is now only blue sky, that and Campese's back vanishing towards the try line. When Campese plays at his best, it's not about strategy or tactics or control. It's about surrender. State of grace, indeed.[16]

But if there was a grace on the field, there was a distinct lack of grace in some of his public commentary off it. This, too, was the age of the noisy braggadocio of American tennis star John McEnroe, whose tirades and racquet-throwing in frustration at umpires' calls represented a new low in an athlete's spleen-venting at officialdom. Campese did not throw tantrums in that vein, but there was very often a raw openness in his public commentary: the heart very much worn on the sleeve. For rugby, it was a double-edged sword. The frank and fearless Campese commentary gave the game much-needed real estate on the sports pages — territory mostly occupied by League and Aussie Rules. On the other hand, it tended to ruffle the game's conservatively preened feathers. Campese, with no filter, evinced sometimes a blithe indifference to the targets of his barbs. To some, it was as endearing as his penchant for free-spirited running; for others, it was the supreme embodiment of what they saw as Campese's selfish, go-it-alone attitude.

Campese was never guilty of foul play in what was an unblemished career; but whatever rules he failed to transgress during a match, he flagrantly defied once the final whistle blew and the microphones appeared. Campese clearly played up to the role of the outspoken maverick, needling oppositions and teammates alike. He was the player of whom it was once famously said — by Wallaby coach Bob Dwyer — that there was 'a wire loose between his brain and his mouth'. Campese's loose lips meant he was as provocative and confounding on air as he was on the field. The tongue never stopped moving, even if his legs occasionally did.

The goosestep

At the heart of the reason Campese is so fondly remembered lies the flair and innovation he brought to his game. Electrifying running was one thing; the use of apparent trickery, quite another. During that debut in New Zealand in 1982, Campese first exhibited on the international stage what was to become known as his signature move: the 'goosestep'. Here again, those writing about the sport found another challenge: the ability to describe it being as elusive as the move itself. If Campese's opposition found it troubling to counter, the journalists likewise struggled to translate it from park to prose. The 'goosestep' was a footloose shuffle that appeared to bamboozle defenders: a half-moment when it appeared Campese stopped running in midair, as if suspended on an invisible highwire, before taking off again at an even quicker pace. To the spectator, it was the essence of a new flamboyance that Campese was bringing to the game: as if he was inviting both opponent and spectator to hold their breath — to wait, even if for a split second — before the next instalment. One scribe discerned perverse plagiarism at play, since Campese had 'marketed the "goosestepping stride" copyrighted by a hundred or more world dictators but utilised it so cleverly on the rugby field with his extraordinary pace'.

So dazzled were some with this innovation that it became the subject of near-scientific inquiry. In 1983, the *Sydney Morning Herald* sent a photographer with a fast-action camera to one of Campese's training sessions to take a series of snaps in an effort to solve the mystery, because to 'the naked eye' the whole move seemed like a 'blur of knees and feet'. They were trying to break it down into something manageable, something, above all, that could be seen. The *Herald*'s Philip Derriman called it 'perhaps the most outstanding example of individual flair in Australian sport today', and, below a series of freeze-framed shots of a goosestepping Campese, took the reader as patiently as he could through each phase of this perplexing feat. 'On approaching a defender, he steps out with his right foot, but then retrieves the foot before it touches the ground. This means, in effect, that he takes two successive paces with his left foot.' That meant, Derriman concluded — with all the authority of a research project's concluding thesis — that the goosestep was 'essentially a dummy step, and its purpose is the same as a dummy pass, to confuse the opposing defenders momentarily'.[17]

Campese was quick to deny being the creator, pointing to its use some years before by a Sydney Rugby League player whose name he could not remember. If the provenance remained unknown, the series of photographs, too, failed to decode its secrets. Even the august television commentator Gordon Bray could sometimes be heard to say, in a state of excited speculation, 'Campese! A goosestep, was it?' Still, that, too, was part of its enduring appeal: the moment so often passed in the blink of an eye. A decade later, the Australian Rugby Union's marketing team made a television jingle about it as a means of attracting more youngsters to watch and play the game. By then, the goosestep had become an indelible part of Campese's cult-like following.

This goosestep was to Campese what the 'flipper' delivery was to become for cricketing leg-spin bowler Shane Warne, and not only because it, too, contained that sudden fizz of speed as the ball leapt from the pitch. As the hallmark of Campese's unique style, it has claims to be placed alongside other sporting innovations of the twentieth century: Englishman Dick Fosbury's 'flop' — an entirely new way of high-jumping; Russian gymnast Yelena Shushunova's gold medal routine at the 1988 Olympics, which introduced the 'straddle jump to land in front ... also with a half turn'; or skier Jan Boklöv's eye-catching new technique for ski-jumping, where, once airborne, his skis were held in a V-shape rather than parallel, thus lengthening the distance made.

Campese's innovation had the added virtue of bringing a new aesthetic to the game, one that might be best compared with that which Dutch soccer player Johan Cruyff brought to football during a 1974 World Cup match against Sweden. As Teresa Lacerda and Stephen Mumford describe it, the so-called 'Cruyff turn' made it look as if the player had 'feigned to make a pass with his right foot but instead trapped the ball under his standing foot and dragged it back behind him. The feint was so convincing that the defender marking him was completely fooled, chasing where the ball would have gone, and Cruyff was now in the penalty area with ten yards of free space before him.'[18]

As Cruyff himself recalled, 'There are impulses that arise because your technique and tactical knowledge has become so great that your legs are able to respond immediately to what your head wants them to do.'[19] Campese, however, would claim no such instruction from head to toe. He always claimed to be simply going wherever his legs took him. All of this helps explain why Campese was to rugby followers the sporting epitome of Churchill's puzzlement over Russian intentions at the outbreak of the Second World War: 'a riddle, wrapped in a mystery, inside an enigma'.

In the wake of Campese's debut in Christchurch, the *Sydney Morning Herald*'s Evan Whitton observed that the 'heavy thinkers of New Zealand rugby nearly went off their brains trying to describe the little number that David Campese unveiled for the stupefaction of his opponents. Was it … a Hesitation Waltz? A minuet? What?' Whitton, though, got closer than most to its essence:

> What he did was throw a foot out, and then bring it back before it touched the ground. The idea was to anchor his opponent before Campo blasted off round him. So it was a feint like nothing seen before, and it blew poor Stu Wilson, 27, veteran of sixty-nine first class matches for the All Blacks, and billed as the best right wing in the world, right out of the water.[20]

As the former New Zealand All Black Grant Batty observed of Campese after the match, 'That goose step of his is a marvellous touch of showmanship [and] just the sort of thing the game needs … it's that little touch of uniqueness that makes him something special'.[21]

Years later, well after Campese had finished playing,

observers of the game were still trying to pin down precisely how the goosestep had worked — a testament to the resilience of its captivating hold on the rugby public. Writing in 1999, British rugby historian Sean Smith thought Campese used it to 'hurtle towards opponents and then begin taking exaggerated steps which gave the illusion he was slowing, when, in fact, he was speeding up. It was like a turbo charge and practically impossible to stop.'[22] And the esteemed Scottish commentator Bill McClaren called it a 'hitch kick ... which checked defenders'. McClaren, too, was convinced that Campese himself didn't know how he did it: 'He'd just be running along when suddenly there was a kind of one-and-a-half, two-and-a-half step.' The local Queanbeyan newspaper stamped its very locality on the move ... calling it 'Campese's struggletown shuffle', naming it after the colloquial term so many affixed to the town itself.[23] Seen in that light, it was simply proof positive that the local boy was doing good, and quite literally getting ahead.

An Australian age

The kind of exhilaration that Campese brought to Rugby Union reflected in its own way the very times in which he played: Australia's 1980s, an age that has come to be associated with sweeping economic reform and rapid social, economic, and technological change, not to mention the meteoric rise — and often equally rapid fall — of the entrepreneur, or chancer. Almost at the same time that

Campese exploded onto the international rugby scene, and only a year after audiences leapt off the cinematic precipice in Snowy River country, a newly elected Labor government led by prime minister Bob Hawke and treasurer Paul Keating were to take Australians over a very different kind of edge. This one was fiscal, psychological, and cultural, leading the electorate towards a new economy more deeply integrated into the international marketplace and its own regional backyard.

These were political adventures of an entirely different kind for Australians, and especially for a Labor Party. They produced different responses. For many, glee at the final breaking down of the tariff wall; for others, anxiety as the local and national steadily gave way to the supposedly unstoppable momentum of international imperatives. Paul Keating's definition of his own political style as 'all downhill, one ski, and no poles' could have been channelling both Banjo Paterson's hero and David Campese. The comment could hardly have been more reflective of that era's prevailing mood — a headlong, near-carefree embrace of adventure, but adventure not without its risks.

Later in his career, as prime minister, Keating was to confess that 'in this game, it's all thrills and spills. One hopes for more thrills than spills, but there are spills around — you have got to avoid them if you can. You can't always.'[24] The comments were not only a coda for the Keating style, but reflective, too, of his self-confessed crazy-brave political ethos: an approach that brought as many critics as it did admirers.

Like Keating and the man from Snowy River taking

their respective audiences off the summit, Campese did the same, metaphorically, each time he took the ball. Together with the thrills of his sometimes slalom-type runs through defenders left strewn in his wake, there were also spills and mistakes in a career that would take the rugby public to the very edge of their seats, and, sometimes, to the outer limits of their patience. As Campese himself was to say subsequently, 'I like to take a lot of risks. It's as if I'm on a tightrope. I can either do some good things or go the other way. You don't know what I'm going to do. I don't know what I'm going to do. I'm living all the time on that line.'[25]

It was as if he was willing the spectator to hop up onto that very line with him. Few could possibly dispute that Campese was one of those players who forced a suspension of belief for those watching on, followed by an inquisition into what had unfolded the moment he took the ball. The verdict was, habitually, instantaneous: effusive praise for his brilliance; searing condemnation for the failures. They were always with him 'on that line', but, as this book will show, never when he came off it.

Even allowing for the fact that one can draw too tightly the links between popular, political, and sporting cultures, there is nevertheless a thread of risk, exuberance, and sheer daring that unites these three moments in Australia's 1980s. Just as an old legend of the Australian bush was being reworked to suit the demands of a modernising world, so the country was being catapulted into a new era with a speed and pace unlike any previous period in its history. And so, too, did Campese seem to relish the title of 'flair merchant', bringing a 'flutter of excitement' to a sport that could so easily be bogged down in grinding forward play or the monotony of kicking the ball from one end of the field to the other. 'I love the buzz when I get the ball,' Campese once said, 'because I'm the guy who does things differently.'[26] And Campese's was a precious and precocious difference: a beacon to appreciate the breathtaking skills of a searing run; a flashing warning light, too, that things could sometimes go awry.

That mixture itself seemed to fit the times, for in the 1980s, old certainties were again coming under challenge; older voices and styles were giving way to newer trends and brash upstarts. The swashbucklers' moment had once more arrived. If it wasn't businessman Alan Bond winning the America's Cup, it was the era in which the country watched with mouths agape at the rise and fall of those figures who were the catalysts, and ultimately the casualties, of the 'wheeler-dealer' culture, such as Christopher Skase and Robert Holmes à Court. It was the decade of new money, corporate greed, extravagance, and wealth.

Keating and Campese were also, in their own respective ways, the carriers of this cavalier spirit. Both were taking on establishments: for Keating, it was a party and a country wedded to older ideas of economic management and moored to older cultural worlds; for Campese, a rugby ethos resting blithely on the private school boater and the Harris tweed of university, those recalcitrant bastions of privilege praying that the clarion calls of professionalism would simply fade away. Both men went about their task with an eye to style, with an eye to performance, and, when necessary, with blunt rhetorical instruments. In their own way, both portrayed themselves as artists in their chosen profession, even if others saw them as *arrivistes*. Like Keating, Campese operated in a manner akin to EM Forster's description of the modern Greek poet Constantine Cavafy: he was at a 'slight angle to the universe'.

It is precisely this difference that holds the key to the Campese persona. Accepting that all sport appeals in different ways to tribal and aesthetic emotions, Campese's style of play resonated with those who watched him — at the ground or on television — in the most intense way. Campese seemed to run both as an agent of change, as well as an agent of resistance: a player refusing to respect orthodoxy, but at the same time harnessing his own talents to stand at the vanguard of an evolving professional ethos in the game.

He was a loner on and off the field. In a sport that could, especially in that era, be awash in its own boozy stupor, he drank only on the rarest of occasions, and even then, usually not much. And he was a pop-culture hero starring in a team that enjoyed enormous success on the world stage in the 1980s and 1990s, when sport seemed to perform the function of offering an easier, less traumatic way for Australians to enunciate national pride and patriotism. Above all else, Campese would come to represent a spirit of free expression and liberation on the field that this period, in its embrace of freewheeling economic rationalism, ironically seemed set to stifle.

No one individual, of course, whether they are a prime minister or a sporting personality, can carry alone the collective memory of a decade or a period in time. And any attempt to define such a period is in itself a fraught process, captive to the inevitable whims and tastes of those trying to capture such times in condensed form. Images of any given decade now get flashed across television screens so quickly that entire periods of history are rendered in simple caricature. These limitations are especially true in the case of Campese, who played in a team that, while it enjoyed great international success, remained determinedly amateur for much of its era at a time when rival codes were extending their reach and popularity.

Many Australians, if asked to name their sporting highlights of the 1980s, would probably opt for the America's Cup victory in 1983, Pat Cash winning Wimbledon, or Allan Border's tenacious captaincy in lean times for Australian cricket. Many, too, would probably nurture memories of a Rugby League or Australian Rules grand final before a Wallaby World Cup win.

Nevertheless, few would doubt that the excitement Campese generated brought new supporters to rugby, and that his skills attracted a following that bordered on devotion. The Irish Nobel laureate poet Seamus Heaney once said, 'When you write, the main thing is to feel you are rising to your own occasion.'[27] It is the aim of this book to show how David Campese went about doing just that: rising to his own occasion, as well as those occasions created by his times: not with a pen, but with an array of talents that continually dazzled and dazed those lucky enough to see him take the field.

CHAPTER ONE

MOVEMENT

When David Campese published the updated version of his autobiography in 1992, he had just played a major part in helping the Wallabies win the Rugby World Cup the year before, and his international career in the sport was at its peak. But even then, Campese was deeply nostalgic for an earlier, lost golden age — not one from a century before, but a mere decade ago. Despite the dazzling backline play that had just characterised the Wallabies' success in lifting the Webb Ellis trophy for the first time, and over which rugby writers had positively drooled, Campese told Peter Bills, the British journalist who penned his memoirs, that he didn't believe 'Australian back play has ever been as penetrative since Mark Ella retired'. And he added that in the early 1980s there was 'a movement, a desire to run, which was never as convincing after Ella finished. We missed from Ella the natural lead in the way to play that kind of game.'[1]

Never mind that the team's incumbent playmaker, Michael Lynagh, had pulled off what is widely regarded as one of the team's finest moments in that tournament — indeed, in Australian rugby history — to achieve a heart-stopping win in a quarter-final against Ireland that looked all but lost, by playing the very kind of running game that Ella himself applauded. Campese, though, was trying to get to something far deeper, a force that had lain dormant since Ella's departure. He was hinting at the very essence, or philosophy, of a particularly Australian style of backline play.

Ella had retired at the age of only twenty-five at the end of the Grand Slam tour of Britain and Ireland in 1984, and is still regarded as one of the greatest players to wear a Wallaby jersey, if not one of the finest exponents of five-eighth play in the history of the game. So when Campese started his own career in 1982, he was joining an Australian team that had started to express itself in a distinctive way on the field, above all by attacking with the ball in hand. Ella and Campese had an expression for it: 'Never let the ball die.' As Ella himself recalls, 'When Australia began playing its "new" running game in the early 1980s, we took the other countries by surprise. Suddenly, instead of constantly kicking for touch, we were standing flat and close and playing a much faster game.'[2]

To the uninitiated, all of this might sound like the recital of the obvious. Rugby is surely about nothing else, if not running with the ball and trying to do it faster, and with greater finesse and more skill, than your opponents. The sport's dubious yet alluring founding myth — that of the young William Webb Ellis breaking the rules by picking up a soccer ball at Rugby School in 1823 — still serves its purpose in promoting that essential belief about the game's defining purpose.

But Australian rugby, like the country itself, lacks a potent foundational myth. In much of the existing literature about the game, however, one series is given a special prominence: that against New Zealand in 1980. Looking now at the footage from those matches, particularly the two played at the Sydney Cricket Ground in July of that year, it is possible to see a combining of all the elements emblematic of this Australian style of running rugby that Ella discussed and for which Campese clearly longed: a swift symphony of movement so mesmerising that it retains the capacity to sweep the viewer along in a kind of breathless wonder at its honeyed fluency. To revisit the replay now, over forty years later, is to be captured by its simple, compelling power, its display of a seamless harnessing of pace, skill, and athleticism. In a sport increasingly prone to boast about its blanket, unrelenting in-your-face defence, this replay is a tantalising window into a very different kind of game being played in another era.

Campese himself has said that watching Ella in this very series spurred his ambition to play for his country. Here was a moment when the Australian rugby side finally expressed itself in a euphoria of liberation. In these matches, a style of play nurtured at the Randwick Rugby Club in the 1920s and 1930s, then reborn at Matraville High in the 1970s, and subsequently taken to Europe with a national schoolboys' team towards the end of that decade, finally flowered at international Test level. 'We were all young,' said Michael O'Connor, the Wallabies' outside centre in that series. 'We didn't have any seniority problems. We threw caution to the wind. That's the feeling that was generated.'[3] Or, as fullback Roger Gould put it, 'We were a very young team, with no expectations being placed on it.'[4]

And it was precisely this carefree style of a new generation that captured the mood of the times. On that score alone, this passage of play offers a glimpse into rugby's purchase on certain *national* sporting imaginings of that time. The pedantic will point out that 'national' here really only means that swathe of suburbs in Sydney, Brisbane, and Canberra where rugby held popular sway and affection, but for those who witnessed it at the time, that series nevertheless stands as Australian rugby's very own coming-of-age moment. The 'new decade', reflected journalist Bret Harris, was coinciding with 'the rise of Australia as a major power' in world rugby.[5]

The movements came predominantly, and most memorably, in the first and then the third and deciding match of that year's Bledisloe Cup series. Since it was first introduced as the symbol of trans-Tasman supremacy in 1931, the Australian side had only won the trophy on three occasions, in 1934, in 1949 — when in any case many of the first-pick All Blacks were in South Africa — and in 1979, when the New Zealand Rugby Football Union, taking pity on their Australian counterpart's parlous financial position, agreed to a one-off Test for the cup in Sydney to help refill the local game's coffers. It was a decision that New Zealand came to regret, for Australia won the match and held the cup aloft in a gleeful lap of triumph around the Sydney Cricket Ground. The trophy was an enormous silver vessel that rather resembled an upturned bell — booty whose very size seemed a statement in itself of an antipodean desire to be taken seriously.

That 1979 Wallaby victory — one which came from penalties only — had been achieved towards the end of a period in which the Australian side had started to build a measure of international self-respect after decades of indifferent, patchy results, the low point of which was an embarrassing loss to Tonga at Ballymore in 1973. But since then it had beaten England at home in a violent two-Test series in 1975; and, three years later, again at home, one of the greatest-ever Welsh sides by a similar margin. A third Test victory over New Zealand at Eden Park in 1978 was punctured by consecutive losses to the touring Irish in Brisbane and Sydney in 1979, but there was no doubt that a marked improvement in how the game was being coached, most visibly represented by the landmark 1975 report into the standards of Australian rugby by Dick Marks, was starting to have its effect.

What cannot be discounted either in this story is the pervasive atmosphere of 'new nationalism' in Australian culture during the 1970s, the belief that a more robust, authentic sense of national pride was starting to bloom in the wake of rapidly diminishing British rites and rituals. That new mood of self-assertiveness coloured almost every major debate in that period: from foreign affairs to the national anthem, from the institution of the Australian of the Year awards and new honours lists to the need for more distinctively Australian content on television and in cinemas. In sport, it came to be most closely associated with the thunderbolts let loose by Australian fast bowlers Dennis Lillee and Jeff Thompson at their English counterparts; and, some years later, with the *Australia II* victory in the America's Cup yacht race.

A television documentary giving an account of Australian rugby in the 1970s is replete with this language of national self-discovery. Thus the decade is described as a 'fight for recognition on the world stage', with journalist Norman Tasker talking of it as a 'period of awakening'. That mood is more than aptly summed up in Wallaby coach David Brockhoff's instructions to his players before that 1975 series against the visiting English side. They were to 'step forward', he said — refuse to be intimidated. That instruction, reportedly delivered in pre-match speeches that had some players in a state of near frenzy as they ran onto the field, is now more remembered for the swinging arms, wild punches, and free-for-all melees that ensued. But there can be little doubt that there was more than a touch of anti-imperial medicine being dished out to the visitors. As Australian breakaway Ray Price — later a stalwart for the Parramatta Eels Rugby League side — bluntly recalled, 'We weren't just going to take the crap that Australia had been given, being used as doormats or whatever.'

Brockhoff, too, would later reflect that, as a result of his soaring perorations, and the results on the field, 'Australia had been at last been given an image, respectability, pride', comments that claimed for rugby not only self-worth in the eyes of their international peers, but which could easily have been spoken by the political and cultural tribunes of the 'new nationalism' of that period: the Labor prime minister Gough Whitlam, public intellectual Donald Horne, novelist Robert Drewe, and others.[6]

Indeed, so explosive and controversial was the effect of the call to 'step forward' that its use was effectively banned on the Wallabies' subsequent tour to the United Kingdom in 1976, its incitement to violence being too much for prim English regard for the 'spirit of the game'. But that tour, too, was interpreted through a new nationalist lens, with captain Tony Shaw speaking of his disgust at the 'colonial attitudes' visited upon his side when travelling across Britain. 'We were the newcomers,' Shaw said, 'and trying to establish ourselves as a force.'[7]

Seasoned watchers of the game were clearly taking note. In the first Test of the 1980 series against New Zealand, a Wallaby try to win the game was orchestrated by five-eighth Mark Ella after a simple looping run around centre Michael Hawker. As Ella took the ball again, the respected New Zealand scribe Don Cameron watched as the Australian glided 'through the gap, haring on the angle across the rear of the All Black defence'. It was 'done with such marvellous timing and speed', he enthused, 'that Ella had simply to curl to his right, find O'Connor and then [Mick] Martin finished it off with a dramatic dive for the try near the corner'. Cameron was clearly as much caught up in the moment as those around him — so much so, in fact, that the feeling of sheer delirium he described would not have been out of place in *The Joy of Sex*:

> Only then did the roar of triumph catch up with the dazzling speed of the thrust. The whole ground erupted in one shattering explosion of sound. It is one thing to win a Test ... with any kind of try ... But to win a Test with a try of such quality, such speed, such daring, turned it into ecstasy.

After the game — perhaps after his own excitement had somewhat subsided and the editor's deadline beckoned — Cameron bumped into Sir Nicholas Shehadie, the president of the Australian Rugby Union. He had 'drawn himself up in lordly posture' — Shehadie had once been lord mayor of Sydney — and 'solemnly intoned that it was a fine win in an excellent game which would do much for the future good of Australian rugby'. But Cameron was having none of it, and waited for the real Shehadie to emerge:

> Then from that lofty eloquence the dinkum Shehadie, the cauliflower-eared battler, emerged. A vast smile crossed his face, his eyes crinkled back under his thick brows, every pore oozing rugby joy ... 'it's bloody good to beat you bastards', putting that special tone of affection into the great Australian idiom.[8]

And that was Shehadie's own way, of course, of giving voice to a sense that things for Australian rugby were finally coming together.

Now, on a sunny July day in Sydney 1980, the Bledisloe Cup series was poised for its decider after the All Blacks had equalised in the second Test at Brisbane's Ballymore ground. While one journalist recalled 'something special in the air', rugby authorities in Australia seemed hard pressed to know what to do with an occasion of this magnitude. The match program itself could have been something produced for a juniors' game, its quaint cover featuring the two tassled ceremonial caps of the respective countries on a gold background. There was no titanic contest being announced here: just a posh, polite rendering of international competition.

The welcome message from Shehadie was much closer to his former Delphic mayoral tones: a study in understatement, merely suggesting that 'the rugby world will be awaiting the result of this magnificent series with much interest'. It ended with the near-plaintive hope that 'this historic occasion in Australian rugby must benefit both countries' — the imperative tone clearly betraying a sense of hope that the match would help continue to support the future of the game in Australia. Only buried at the bottom of a preview of the game on page 14, and in near-microscopic print, was there an admission of the stakes involved:

The Wallabies have been brought back to earth, the All Black machine is once again rolling with its power pack and more balanced backline, the series is level, the Bledisloe Cup is up for grabs ... it's a promoter's dream.[9]

Here was an amateur sport trying hard not to get too excited about its own product; trying hard, too, to exercise what it saw as appropriate restraint at a moment in which so many believed it was poised to reach new heights.

But it might also be said the promoters in this era were hardly required: the crowd had certainly turned up — nearly 49,000 jammed inside the ground to see the Wallabies win by 26–10, only the fourth time in seventy-seven years of Tests against New Zealand that Australia had won a series. That crowd figure was only 600 below a seventy-three-year-old ground attendance record; captain Tony Shaw confessed later that 'we hardly ever filled the stadiums, but that day they were hanging from the rafters'.[10]

To watch any replay of this kind is the equivalent of being dropped into a time capsule. Easy it is to unselfconsciously become trapped inside that vortex of the sacred that the Sydney Cricket Ground is held to represent in the nation's sporting psychology. But it remains the case that all stadia exude a particular aura, being both a cradle of memory and a cauldron of expectation. Looking at the Sydney Cricket Ground's configuration in the 1980s, what strikes almost immediately is the expanse of openness on the eastern side of the ground. A thronged 'Hill' at that time still sprawls along much of it, interrupted only by the bottle-green roofed 'Bob stand', itself arced gently around towards the members area. That space and sweep of the ground's own horizon seem to lend the atmosphere its very own swirl and hum — the crowd a buzzing mass awaiting the spectacle.

As the *Sun-Herald*'s Dorothy Goodwin recalled on the day, the 'air on the Hill was ready to explode', noting with surprise that most of those there under the age of twenty-five seemed to know the words of 'Road to Gundagai' when the tune was struck up by the military band. They'd paid only five dollars to sit there, she added, but finding a spot to sit — among the 'picnic baskets, half-eaten hot dogs, hands [and] feet' — was another challenge altogether, not to mention that the price of admission provided 'a view of the game but not the players, who were a blur' from that distance, a 'distant race stewed green and gold, then black'.[11] Even if unwittingly, Goodwin had put her finger on a longstanding problem for Australian rugby: their sport was mostly played on oval shaped cricket grounds, and with rugby's rectangular pitch plonked squarely in the middle, the crowd could never really be close enough to the action.

Only those in the stands, then, would have noted the intrusive silhouette of a one-day cricket light angled across the turf, while the turreted members' stand threw down its own colonial-era shadows. At the Hill's back, the cavernous hall of the Commemorative Pavilion hulked, while the gleaming white grandstand of the Sydney Showground had its back turned to its neighbour in wilful impertinence. A green-disced playing surface is ringed by what would now be looked on as primitive advertising hoarding, an archive of an age's heady pleasures: crowds there and at home implored to smoke mild Cravens, drink Tooheys, fill up with Ampol, chew PK gum for its 'taste of action', munch Smiths crisps, and fly Ansett. Wang was advertising its computers and word processors, Honda its new Civic. Four black-and-white striped cardboard corner posts marked longitude and latitude, limp red flags sagged atop the goalposts: no wind to lend them purpose. No team doctors or physiotherapists, either, running onto the ground back then. But the St John's Ambulance staff were there, one of them on the sideline drinking from a blue flask, the version that came with a plastic white cup affixed: a staple of Australian family outings in that era.

The commentary, too, was from another age — the former Wallaby Trevor Allan can be heard heralding a 'valiant' run by Australian fullback Roger Gould, condemning just 'really bad football' when kick-offs did not travel the requisite distance, and stating — with no pretence of sympathy — that 'here's hoping the injury is not serious' as the fallen All Black winger Tim Twigden lay motionless on the ground for what seemed an eternity.[12] With concussion protocols still thirty years into the future, Twigden might as well have been lying in no man's land during the Battle of the Somme.

But from that match it is the image of an unrestrained Australian backline that endures. As the journalist Bret Harris would later write, the 'artistic Australian backs painted a rugby masterpiece across the SCG canvas'.[13] Harris was clearly reaching to get beyond the typical sporting reportage here, seeing the movement of these players as something more than simply a well-drilled team going through its paces: something transcendental. Of the players involved in that series — halfbacks Peter Carson and Philip Cox, five-eighth Mark Ella, centres Michael Hawker and Michael O'Connor, fullback Roger Gould, wingers Mick Martin, Peter Grigg, and Brendan Moon — only the names of Ella and O'Connor would fast trigger sporting memories today — and O'Connor probably more for the fame he was to subsequently make in Rugby League. 'One of the hottest properties in rugby', as his pen portrait in the program said that day, a description to make the rugby purist wince when it is considered that only two years later he would be lost to the game.

But the movements of those players — collectively — has been accorded a near revolutionary weight in the game's history in Australia. The shackles, it seemed, were being broken. Captain Tony Shaw, once more talking the language of the 'new nationalism', said 'we'd come from an environment where we were a little bit restricted, particularly the backs, in what they could do and where they could do it from on the paddock. All of a sudden we had a team that could do anything from anywhere and were prepared to run it from anywhere. So I think the whole attitude of Australian rugby changed.'[14] Here was the belief that a national style 'of our own' was finally being given the chance to imprint itself on the country's sporting consciousness. Only now it was being consciously grafted onto the biggest sporting stage of all, and against the mightiest opponent of all: the New Zealand All Black foe. For the Wallabies to have beaten the world's best — and to achieve it on the Sydney Cricket Ground, no less — was viewed as nothing less than a glorious national arrival.

One of the television cameras broadcasting the game that day was positioned at the Randwick end of the ground — probably around where the old Sheridan stand used to be. And in one of the clips from that match, what appears to be approaching the viewer, at pace, is a phalanx of Wallabies emerging from the gloom, out from that late-afternoon darkness made by the long shadows cast over the Paddington end of the ground by the roof of the Bradman stand. As the Australian backline starts to move forward at top speed, it resembles a line of hoplites advancing rapidly up field, as if they were Athenians fanning onto the plain at Marathon. But this is no rigid battle formation — for as the ball begins to move along the backline, each set of arms appears to be a series of pendula, timed to sway almost in the same style and at pre-programmed intervals, as each player transmits the ball from one to the other, each pass forming its own discrete, but short, parabola to the player outside. So seamless is the transition of the ball, so effortlessly does each player appear to swing his arms out in front and across the body, while at the same time gliding into open space, that the ball itself is momentarily lost: it is the movement of arms that catches the eye. Little wonder such movement was more colloquially known as 'elephant trunk' passing.

It all started with Mark Ella. Once asked by journalist Evan Whitton what distinguished Ella's particular playing style, the former Wallaby Cyril Towers, himself often referred to as the 'father of the running game' in Australia, said that 'Ella runs from the shoulders down, with the fingers, hands and arms completely relaxed, he takes the ball on one side and passes before the foot comes down again'.[15] This brings to mind the reflection of Carwyn James, the coach of the victorious 1971 British Lions to New Zealand, on the requirements of a good rugby player, that 'it is the open hand of the artist that fingers the ball, and the energy to pass it comes from the wrists and not from his arms, and his every movement is clean and complete'.[16] By half time the Australian backs had scored three tries — in the words of a young Gordon Bray, the 'New Zealanders were really being stretched by the pace of these Australians'. The 'young Australian backs', he added, were 'running riot'.

In his reflections on the 'art of running rugby', written sometime after his own playing days were over, Mark Ella gave expression to this achievement of what he called the 'flowing game'. Its perfection was a kind of outrageous perversion, giving the appearance of being an entirely natural way of playing the sport, akin to children simply doing what they wanted down at the local park, running carefree, at will. There was certainly an element of that, but this style took an enormous amount of coaching and discipline, and it came from a type of backline play first exhibited by New Zealand sides in the 1920s and duly adapted to the Australian game later that same decade by Towers.

It would be forging entirely new myths to suggest that the Australian sides in the intervening half-century played only a stolid, predictable game with no attempt to run the ball from anywhere on the field. Or that the famous Welsh teams of the 1970s, or the French sides of the late 1960s and

1980s, both remembered for backlines glittering with some of the most brilliant running stars of all time — the brothers Guy and André Boniface, Serge Blanco, JPR Williams, Gareth Davies, and Phil Bennett, to name a few — did not thrill or entertain, too. Nevertheless, a set of factors came together in the late 1970s and early 1980s that enabled this particular group of players to perform it at the international level in such a way as to see it becoming associated with the country itself, or at the very least with an Australian style of rugby.

In his book, Ella laid it out clearly: 'You must be able to catch under pressure, pass under pressure and run at the correct angle in support.' All of this, to the lay reader, simply sounds like the very basics of a sport, but what Ella was getting at has to be understood in the context of how his schoolboy rugby coach at Matraville High, Geoff Mould — himself influenced by Cyril Towers — was coaching the game in the late 1970s.

'At Matraville,' Ella recalled, 'we played a close-quarters support game, standing flat as well as close, so all we had to do was hand the ball to each other ... we played as if the ball belonged to us, as if we owned it and were entitled to keep it for as long as we liked.' Performed at pace, Mould had introduced a concept to that team called 'sympathetic passing', the practice of 'popping the ball up to your teammate in a way that makes it as simple as possible for him to catch'. The alignment may have also reflected the influence of Rugby League — it being the more popular sport at the school prior to Mould introducing rugby.

The key point was its sharp contrast to what Ella saw as the prevailing system of how the game was played in private schools, where 'GPS teams in Sydney were taught to do firm passes' and to stand 'as much as ten metres apart' in the backline so they had to 'fire the passes at each other to make the distance'.[17] It is hard not to see in this statement a reflection of class attitudes and their interaction with this style of play: by implication, the state system had its players closer to the advantage line, closer together and performing at greater speed and with greater accuracy. Implicitly, they were hungrier, prepared to take more risks, inherently more skilful, eager to get ahead. Those less imaginative in the private schools, however, were depicted as still operating very much on the English model — standing deep, at a safe distance from real pressure, and so far away from the action that virtual telegrams needed to be sent in advance of the pass. Still, Michael Hawker, a product of the elite Shore School in Sydney, and later Michael Lynagh, Tim Horan, and Jason Little, all products of private schools in Queensland, became adept exponents of this theory once coached in its ways.

Ella supported his explanation with a series of diagrams to show how this flat, close backline formation worked — drawn with all the fastidious care of the military strategist — its essence being 'great skill, great discipline and great confidence ... each the product of years of practice and experience'. But the real significance of Ella, Hawker, and O'Connor showing these skills at Test level was that they had done it before — and with Mould as coach — on the

Australian schoolboys' tour of Europe, the United Kingdom, and Ireland in 1977–78. As Ella noted, 'Many of the backline moves that the Australian team used at Test level in the early 1980s ... were moves that we had used back in the Matraville under fifteens. We just took them with us as we moved up the ladder — to the Australian schoolboys, then to Randwick, and finally, to the Australian side.'[18] This might also be seen as the first fruits of Australian coaching success.

On that day in 1980, however, as Australia recorded its biggest-ever victory over New Zealand, Ella recalls that 'everything we did just turned to gold, and it was one of those magic days'. No wonder one reporter at the ground described the game as a 'triumphal march'.[19] Such appraisals, while accurate, are still to be treated with some caution: the euphoria was surely relative to the disappointments that had dotted the previous decade. This match was no wall-to-wall demonstration of faultless play — few matches ever are — and it certainly had its fair share of dropped balls, missed field goals, scrappy moments, and mistakes. Whatever those slips, however, there was something significant to be discerned in the crowd singing 'Waltzing Matilda' with 'gusto', according to the commentators — it can be heard on the replay — and this with more than twenty minutes remaining in the Test with the score at 26–6 in Australia's favour.

As Australian player Greg Cornelsen told Philip Derriman, 'It was unheard of in any sport for Australians to be actually singing, and for the whole crowd to be

singing Waltzing Matilda was just remarkable and fantastic
… a lasting memory.'[20] Cornelsen was probably thinking
more of the kinds of crowds he'd played before in Britain,
such as those at Cardiff Arms Park or Twickenham, both
cathedrals of folk nationalism and choral fervour. Australian
sporting crowds have never been known to be laconic, but
singing — especially for a Rugby Union crowd — was
indeed nothing short of remarkable. Cornelsen's surprise,
no doubt, also emanated from the fact that, in this period,
the Australian government had brought back the singing of
'God Save the Queen' as Australia's national anthem, with
'Waltzing Matilda' classified as one of four national songs to
be sung when Australians felt that the occasion demanded
it. Clearly, this was one of them.

Ella gives a sense of what that performance generated in
an eager public:

> Suddenly, the Australian newspapers were writing about
> the dawn of a new era in Australian rugby. They raved
> about the way we played the game, about our running
> rugby … The Australian crowds loved to see backs
> running the ball and they soon developed an appetite for
> it. We in the Australian team sensed this and felt we had
> to give the public more of it. We had created a market for
> the running game, and now we were under pressure to
> keep up the supply.[21]

This performance created a market in more ways than
one — and not just a hankering among crowds for more

ball-running. Australian rugby officials, with all-too-painful memories of having to reach deep into empty pockets in the previous few years, forecast a profit of $200,000 from the match, and had even forked out the cash to allow players to have their wives and girlfriends stay at a hotel in Sydney for the night of the game. By today's standards, these were small profits for the administrators, and the barest of privileges for players and their beloveds, especially given what the professional cohort have come to expect today. But they do show a Union body at least aware of the growing sentiment that players were sacrificing much in order to represent their country. As Don Cameron later wrote, 'You get the impression Australian rugby is beginning to surge along a well-planned groove ... all the coaching and planning and promotion has now left Australia with a team on the verge of greatness.'[22]

Ella was right about the press being wildly enthusiastic in the wake of this Test match. So enamoured were some that they concluded the game's geopolitical balance of power itself was shifting, even if only across the Tasman sea. The very youth of the side, coupled with the manner of their play, was a potent brew. One journalist could barely contain himself, even going so far as to suggest that the 'Bledisloe Cup looks perfectly at home here'; another quoted a former All Blacks coach saying that Australia was now at the 'top of the rugby world'.[23] All such statements ladled even more expectations upon the players, and, of course, ignored the historical fact that the ledger of rugby supremacy, where New Zealand was concerned, remained heavily stacked against the Wallabies. But memories are inevitably shorter when standing on the cusp of what seems like a glowing future.

No Australian player could easily forget the reception to this win, inked in the next day's press. Headlines such as 'Come on the world! — All Blacks conquerors look set for golden era', 'Australia in Test blitz', 'Australia's Cup', and 'All Blacks crushed' lent the rhetoric of battle and military victory to the occasion. It was, of course, nothing new for a mostly one-eyed press corps to blow the trumpets. They saw in that eighty minutes both the 'ushering' in of a new era and a coming of age, 'at last'.[24]

While the Australian forwards were given their due, it was the backline play that had caught the eye. In *The Australian*, Phil Wilkins announced that 'Australia has a Rugby Union team capable of outrunning any in the world.' Only South Africa stood in front of them. Wilkins suggested they'd 'have to win in the forwards', for 'they would never beat Australia in the backs'. In the *Sun-Herald*, Russel Eldridge was sure that it was the 'lusty boyishness of the Australian game' that had won the day, while his colleague Brian Mossop took it further, heralding the backline's 'style and flair seen all too seldom in international rugby'. The comparison Mossop made to their 'flat-footed, wooden and butter fingered' New Zealand opponents only lifted the Australians onto a higher pedestal.[25]

However, Evan Whitton, the editor of the *National Times*, took the prize for the requisite touch of literary flair that took the occasion into another realm entirely. Whitton's column began with a quote from Lewis Carroll's nonsense poem, 'Jabberwocky', which had appeared in *Through the Looking Glass*, the sequel to *Alice's Adventures in Wonderland*. 'O frabjous day, Callooh! Callay!' sang Whitton in his opening lines, claiming — perhaps hoping — that there wasn't a 'heart out of the 48,000 at the Cricket Ground ... that didn't echo Lewis Carroll' as the Australian win was recorded. Quoting directly from the poem, Whitton found the lyrical register to bring the movements of the players to life:

One two! One, two! And through and through,
The vorpal blade went snicker snack.

And in case of any doubt in the reader's mind, those 'vorpal blades on these occasions were the dazzling Australian backs who made the holes for the Townsville flyer, Peter Grigg'. He could have quoted the final two lines of that stanza — 'he left it dead, and with its head, he went galumphing back', for in Whitton's mind the Wallabies had slain the All Black Jabberwocky. Whitton, too, was not averse to mining the glossary of the 'new nationalism', for his conclusion was that, 'after a century, Australian rugby has finally thrown off its protracted adolescence and pinned its faith on a running game by a great backline'.[26]

In his book *Death in the Afternoon*, written in the 1930s about bullfighting in Spain, Ernest Hemingway said that 'without the sun, the best bullfighter is not there. He is like a man without a shadow.' There is something to the way in which Sydney's bright yet cold winter light on that day in July 1980 appeared to illuminate a Wallabies side emerging from a period of relative darkness. What counts here is not the creation of a new, heroic myth, but rather the recognition that a young team had been brought together at the highest level of the game, and in a way that did announce an Australian way of running the ball — a style that over the next decade was to give Australian rugby supporters some of their most memorable moments. It is also to acknowledge the early success of a system of national coaching and talent identification that would continue to provide the essential building blocks for the national game over the following twenty years.

It was this team, too, albeit one chastened by a disappointingly unsuccessful British Isles tour in 1981, that a young David Campese, fresh from blazing a trail across suburban grounds in Queanbeyan and Canberra, was about to enter. Just over two years after this particular Test match, and playing at the same ground, Campese was to score a try for the Australian Under-21 side against New Zealand that was to remain long in the minds of those who were there that day. And he was to touch down directly in front of the Sir Donald Bradman stand.

CHAPTER TWO

FREEDOM

Writing after his retirement from international rugby, David Campese advised those still playing the game to 'squeeze every last minute out of your ... career because, as the old adage goes, you are a long time retired. You miss it when you give it away.'[1] Campese was not the first sporting great — nor will he be the last — to look back with nostalgia on his playing days, to invest his own past with the kind of aura that others might search antiquity to find. As the cricket writer Neville Cardus once wrote, 'The Golden Age is always well behind us ... we catch sight of it with young eyes, when we see what we want to see.' Cardus's biographer, Duncan Hamilton, claims that his subject knew the difficulty of trying to 'convince one generation about the merits of a world to which it hadn't borne witness'.[2] If that was difficult for a sportswriter, it seems all the more herculean a task for some former players. There is a sense that Campese wanted time to stand still — odd for a player whose signature was sizzling speed and a zapping sidestep. But there is no doubt that once he finished playing, Campese could not easily satisfy his longing for the 'challenge and the adrenalin rush all rolled into one' that he said had defined his time in representative rugby.[3]

Like so many former champions, Campese's calendar after he stopped playing quickly brimmed with hospitality events and speaking engagements, the writing of newspaper columns, and commitments on television and radio. Both the pen and the tongue were wielded with the same rapier's thrust that he'd brought to his on-field play, but from his own writings what emerges time and again is that nothing could dull the ache of not being out there, on the field and in the arena. So there is much to be read into his confession, made around the time of the Rugby World Cup being hosted in Australia in 2003, that 'if I had my time over I would swap it all to be on the rise again as a teenager, to be making my first tour of New Zealand, to have a 15-season career with the Wallabies all laid out ahead of me'.[4]

It is worth looking more closely, then, at those very years in which Campese began to make his first mark on the game, when the fields of Queanbeyan and Canberra hosted a precocious talent blossoming for the first time. Campese has said that never was he to enjoy playing rugby as much as he did in these years — more, indeed, than those in which he wore an Australian jumper. In his recollections of the time, there is a purity to that period that says much, not only about the formative influence of club rugby on his career, but also about the underlying reason he played the game — namely, for enjoyment. It's here that Campese is beginning to learn about self-expression on the sporting field, and about the capacity of his athletic skills to give new meaning to his emerging persona.

Campese's story, rising from what he called 'that little town of Queanbeyan' to a first Wallaby cap, also shows a Rugby Union ecosystem working: identifying talent — even if not from the traditional strongholds of New South Wales and Queensland — pushing it through the system, and, when it met a certain resistance from local selectors, overriding it for the good of the national game. It would probably shock readers to learn that more Test players in this era came from rural Australia,[5] and while Queanbeyan was hardly the bush — indeed, it was often dismissed as a 'Cindarella' town to the neighbouring national capital — it remains proof that a player with Campese's class, boasting no private school pedigree, no pre-ordained procession through New South Wales Combined High Schools or Australian Schoolboy representative sides — could be selected to play for the Wallabies. As one chronicler of Campese's trajectory put it much later, 'At 17 he was playing fourth grade for Queanbeyan. Within two years he was lining up against the All Blacks. Some player.'[6]

The son of working-class parents, Campese left school at sixteen and played more Rugby League than Union in his youth, before rocketing to the international rugby scene, and stardom, within a mere three years. And he was doing so when Queanbeyan was — still is — a Rugby League town.

One of its local historians claims it would be difficult to determine which code had the greater following, since 'both the Union "Whites" and the League "Blues" were averaging about the same number of column inches in the *Queanbeyan Age* sporting pages over the years'.[7] But the creation of the Canberra Raiders in the early 1980s, which headquartered at the local Seiffert Oval, shows that at the time Campese was making his mark, momentum was building towards the formation of a team to compete in the New South Wales Rugby League competition.

That journey from fourth grade to a Wallaby Test berth is part of the Campese story, but not in a way that slips predictably into a rags-to-riches tale. Rather, it stands as that time in his career when Campese, emerging as a local rugby star, was simply allowed to have his head, to express himself most fully before the constraints that come with higher honours imposed — or tried to impose — new codes of responsibility on his play, new meanings of what was acceptable to try on the field, and what wasn't. It was Campese's first time 'To wonder', to quote TS Eliot, 'Do I dare?' and 'Do I dare disturb the universe?'

Dare and disturb he did. As one of Campese's coaches in Queanbeyan, Bob Hitchcock, later recalled of this period: 'We saw him before the rest of the world did ... we got to see the unfettered Campo ... [and] when we saw him no one had put any harnesses on him.'[8] It is a tantalising insight into a young player clearly in the process of discovering the extent, and at times the limits, too, of his talent. But it also says much about how those supporting his rise through the representative ranks retained a kind of ownership of Campese, felt an enduring privilege of having seen what no one else could ever again see: to have been present at the creation of a special player. Given that Campese was so often praised for the unorthodox, cavalier spirit he brought to a game better known for its clear patterns, straight lines, and pre-programmed phases of play, this glimpse — for it is only a glimpse — of what local writers often called the 'young Campese' or 'dashing David' is all the more compelling.

The 'kid from Queanbeyan'

Campese defined his own life philosophy as having a 'free perspective, a freedom which no one can take away'.[9] That, in itself, says something about a childhood in which he tried his hand at all sports, and at a young age showed promise in golf, cricket, Little Athletics, and Aussie Rules. It also speaks to how the collective embrace of family, community, and club allowed him to express those skills, and therefore himself, in the most unrestrained way. All art, and all sport as an art form in its own right, constitutes a vehicle of human expression, a blend of the aesthetic and the competitive. Campese's first flourish as a rugby artist — the newspapers often referred to him as 'Mr Magic' — and his initial burst onto the local scene present a thrilling entrée to the career that would subsequently go on to influence the way in which the game of rugby itself was played, watched, and appreciated. All of the ingredients that would characterise his international career — his relationship with the crowd, the becoming of a drawcard in his own right, the expectation that he could, would, and should pull off the miraculous every time he touched the ball, and the kind of pressure being applied on him to perform, week in and week out — were just as much part of his Queanbeyan days as they were of his subsequent international career.

Campese grew up in the house his father built. Gianantonio Campese, from the village of Montechio Precalcino, near Venice, had arrived in Australia in 1952 as part of the post-war migration boom from southern Europe. A French polisher by trade, Gianantonio, or Tony as he quickly became known, had at first worked on that great icon of national post-war reconstruction, the Snowy-Hydro scheme. He also lent his expertise to the construction of one of the newer monumental sculptures in the nation's capital — the Australian–American memorial that soars skywards in front of the Defence Department offices on Russel Hill. Campese recalls his father telling him that he scratched his initials into the eagle's wings atop that very column. Tony married a local girl, Joan, who lived on the same street and worked as a cleaner. It was the same street where Tony would construct the family home, replete with a market garden overflowing not only with vegetables, which the children would often sell to neighbours, but wine grapes, too. Their presence led to visitations by the local police on account of the suspicion that Tony was involved in bootlegging.

By the time David was born in 1962, close to half of Queanbeyan's population had non-English-speaking backgrounds — the majority of them being Italians,

Germans, Greeks, and Macedonians. Campese's early life, then, took place against the backdrop of a rapidly changing Australia, one moving gradually away from an insistence on newly arrived migrants assimilating to the 'Australian way of life' — within the clearly defined parameters of a society anchored in British-race patriotism — to one beginning a tortuous loosening of its race-based identity and adopting instead a commitment to multiculturalism. By the 1960s, members of the local Italian community in Queanbeyan had, like other migrant groups, not only established themselves as part of a vibrant, multi-ethnic township, but they had formed clubs and establishments to give their presence a bricks-and-mortar reality: in 1959 a Marco Polo Club was founded, and by the early 1970s it had its own fully licensed premises.

That is not to equate numbers or mere presence with widespread acceptance. Campese's name was continually mangled by the local press. He was 'Capese', 'Campeese', 'Campers', or at other times was afforded a Spanish air with the grand appellation of 'El Campo'. Like many children with a European background, his schoolmates teased him as a 'wog'. It is not known precisely when the Australian penchant for suffixing a foreign name like Campese with an 'o' to turn it into 'Campo' first surfaced. In any case, Anglo names were hardly immune from the same declensions. But in this case the Australianising of the Italian surname was surely ignorant of its returning 'Campese' closer to its linguistic roots — the Latin word *campus*, like the Italian *campo*, means, appropriately enough, 'field'.

Campese seems to have been little affected by the taunts and teasing. A documentary of his life was perhaps stretching it to equate the development of his evasive running skills to being bullied in the playground, Campese having supposedly learned to dodge and weave his way through the local rat-pack of bullies. Instead, Campese recounts what really amounts to a classic Australian childhood. You had the 'roads to yourself', he recalled, with 'not many cars around'. The streets became stadia, cricket pitches, running tracks. His mother and father were the 'furthest thing you've ever seen from pushy parents', he would write in his autobiography. Schoolwork never grabbed him; but sport — any sport from the smorgasbord laid out — clearly did. In the classroom, he would 'count down the minutes until I could get a football, a cricket bat or a golf club in my hands'.[10]

While this self-described 'kid from Queanbeyan' displayed an amazing sense of confidence in his early years — one that was continually the subject of comments from the first journalists who reported on him, not to mention from teammates who played alongside him — Campese never baulked at revealing his sensitivity, never saw the need to hide the heart worn on the sleeve. Given the kind of criticism that was meted out to him by press and peers alike over the course of his career, it is perhaps not surprising to learn that a Rugby League coach's denunciation of him at the age of fifteen stung in a way that has not only lingered into adulthood, but pushed him to commit more fully, and indeed, forever, to Rugby Union. In the wake of playing in an Under-16 Rugby League grand final for the Queanbeyan Blues against

Belconnen, Campese was blamed for missing crucial tackles that, so his coach pointed out, lost his team the game.

Remembering himself as a 'fairly skinny kid' who was a 'bit scared about going into contact situations too hard', Campese was unsure at the time how to respond. Notwithstanding the attempt to stitch up 'any internal bleeding', he could not overcome the rebuke. It ate into him. What he recalls, too, about the Rugby League culture in the town was that he simply didn't warm to its ways, particularly to the peer pressure. He looked askance at its culture: the 'biff-bang of League and the grog ... turned me off', he would later write. He was not up for playing the 'macho-man' at parties, with teammates 'thinking themselves ever so clever if they can hold a pint and swill it'. All of this amounted to a situation, as he put it, in which he simply 'didn't fit into the picture very well'.[11]

Those reflections bring out a number of themes in Campese's early life, and not just a fear of failure, or the loneliness that came from a decision not to swim in or even alongside the current. Campese turned Henry Thoreau's words on their head — it wasn't so much that he did not keep pace with his companions, it was that he outpaced them, literally, by hearing a different drummer and stepping to his own music. They also clearly reveal a determination to stand apart — if only 'to achieve something' in his sporting life.[12] But they might point, too, to a deep-seated belief that he never really fitted into the brazen masculine bravado that permeated the culture of Rugby Union either. It might have shown even then that the individualism he so brilliantly expressed on the field, and which he clearly cherished off it, was inevitably going to rub uneasily against a sporting milieu that is at times necessarily, at others bloody-mindedly, predicated on the power of the collective effort. Not for Campese the 'rugger-bugger' culture of the clubhouse or the post-match painting of the town.

These early years planted the seeds of his own professionalism in match preparation — an avoidance of alcohol, the adherence to a strict diet, the devotion to a daily training regimen. Campese had even been taken aside by one of the coaches at the Queanbeyan club, Peter Morton, a former rugby representative for New South Wales, and told in no uncertain terms that he was never again to be seen with a beer in hand. 'Peter was also a black belt in karate,' Campese recalled, 'and he told me I had too much talent to waste. Out of sheer respect for him, and as a raw youngster, there was simply no way I was going to defy him.'[13]

He was the very epitome, even then, of the desire for self-improvement that bordered on — at times even transcended — the obsessive. It was as if the regimentation he imposed on himself in preparing for the sport allowed him the opportunity to discard the very regimentation so often demanded by a team game. Even amid the euphoria of his selection for the Australian side in 1982, as the beer flowed at the Queanbeyan Rugby Club at a special function to celebrate his achievement, one of his teammates quietly observed that 'it was probably not clearly stated that Campese had worked hard to reach the highest level in the game. Many a lonely night was spent at Taylor Park ... kicking for goals, teaching himself how to kick with his left foot.'[14]

Nearly all accounts in the sporting-hero genre feel a compulsion to reveal what might be called the creation, or origin, story: the game or match where the talent is first discovered, the photo of the young star captured for posterity, the great future predicted. There is a reading back into the life of a destiny that perhaps had been pre-determined, divined by unknown forces. A momentum all its own is generated as the player ascends from a junior side to national and then global recognition. Today, the advent of the iPhone means that many footballing stars have had their entire junior careers faithfully recorded by a parent, later uploaded to YouTube as proof positive of a star-in-the-making saga.

In the case of David Campese, there remains no video of his earliest playing days, but there is one photograph in particular that stands out. In it, he is at full stretch playing for the Queanbeyan Under-9s Rugby League side in 1971. The ball is cradled in one arm, the fingers spread evenly across the leather ball: he looks like he will never let go of it. His thick, dark hair is swept back by the wind, his eyes are closed, his tongue peeping out. The jersey is tucked in, his socks pulled up and neatly folded over. Behind him, a posse of beaten defenders scrambles to keep up: some stationary, others just puffed. At the very moment the camera shutter snaps shut, neither of Campese's feet are on the ground. He is at full stretch, the balance perfectly weighted. He might as well be flying. This is a child in his element, running free.

One paragraph in the local paper, too — but a strikingly

accurate one — from around the same time has also come to be viewed as an augury. Campese's reputation was already doing the rounds of the local grounds in the early 1970s, and in 1972 the editor of the *Queanbeyan Age*, Barry Gilman, went to watch Campese play for the local Under-10s Rugby Union team. Writing a round-up column called 'Our Town' under the byline of the 'Town Crier', Gilman had been clearly taken by what he saw, for, though the senior Queanbeyan team had thrashed their opponents 53–6 that Sunday (in what he described as a 'real shot in the arm for the club'), the 'player of the day' was David Campese, the 'great little five-eighth' who was 'instrumental in helping the junior side beat Canberra Grammar Under-10s 12–0'. Gilman thought that 'Capese' had 'all the natural ability of a Test rugby player and it is my prediction that he will be one of the greats of the game in another decade'.[15] Given that Campese did, in fact, gain selection for Australia on that precise timeline, it is not hard to see why Gilman's paragraph has taken on such significance.

'To exercise his talents'

One of the selectors at the Queanbeyan Whites Rugby Club remembers clearly Campese's arrival on the scene. He brought with him the trademark confidence, even arrogance. As Peter Debenham recalled:

> Early in 1979 I was confronted at training by a very slight lad who I understood had played Under-15s or Under-16s

the previous year. He confirmed that I was a selector then informed me that if he didn't get a run this Saturday he was off to join another club. Consternation!! His parents supported his desire to move up to grade football and we all agreed on a starting season in Fourth Grade where we fielded a strong side of veteran players many of whom had played 100 first-grade games or more of rugby.

As Debenham recalled, 'The excitement was there every time he touched the ball and we soon gave up running back to support "the kid" as that only meant he had to weave his way through us as well as opposition players and then we had to try and catch up.'[16]

What emerges from the match reports of Campese's early playing days is a picture of an emerging style, but above all else of Campese's desire to strike the boldest of notes virtually every time he took the field. All of the ingredients that would come to characterise how future reporters would write about him were already there. Words sought to adorn, to grasp the special nature of the talent on display. A Campese teammate from that era stressed that he 'created so much space' for everyone else, and that he would 'attack from anywhere'; time and again in the match reports, it was Campese's individual performances that captured attention.[17] His play was 'classy' and 'made the difference'; he was 'ubiquitous', 'elusive', 'gifted', and a 'wonder'; and his running was a cause for 'scintillating excitement'. And when the thesaurus was exhausted, the pictures accompanying the stories would often carry the simplest, most basic, of captions: David Campese was simply a 'top player'.

Campese was doing all this in a Canberra competition that, while not considered to be at the standard of its Sydney or Brisbane counterparts, had certainly produced its fair share of national talent — among them Michael O'Connor and, before him, Peter Ryan, David Grimmond, Stuart McDougall, and John Weatherstone. The 'Mighty Whites' in Queanbeyan, established in 1954, won their first premiership five years later, and were, according to historian Jack Pollard, a 'force' in Australian Capital Territory rugby, backed by a licensed club — not something that all Canberra clubs could boast.[18] This competition, too, had its rivalries and tribalism. The sneer could work both ways. Queanbeyan players, like everyone in the competition, hated the much-fancied and much-wealthier Royals club. A trip to play the Australian National University was considered almost an overland journey 'to the land of the intellectuals'. Games against the Royal Military College were an opportunity to muscle up to the Duntroon cadets.

To help explain Campese's impact on this competition, it might be useful — even if ambitious — to make a vast leap backwards, all the way to late-nineteenth-century France. For Campese's pattern of play might be seen as something more akin to the style of rugby played in France in that era, when 'rugby was not so much a collective sport as an individual one, pitting the intelligence of the athlete against the anonymous strength of the group'. This was about the elevation of elegance over brawn. The rugby player of that era, observes French scholar Thierry Teret, was a 'fast-moving athlete who knew how to fake and spin around, to trip and break away'. And it was on this approach to the game that French reporters 'showered praise'.[19]

But Queanbeyan was no Paris.

As Campese delivered a flair and elan of a kind not often seen in this local competition, it was hardly surprising that he, too, drew plaudits. But he also felt pressure's heavy hand for the first time. After playing first grade for only two months in 1980, he found that predictions about his future were already starting. When he was promptly selected for the Australian Capital Territory Under-21 side, the *Queanbeyan Age* declared that Campese 'had the stamp of class and is the sort of player who can turn a game with unpredictable running and clever switches of play ... Sydney rugby people will see the similarity between Campese and former Wallaby Russell Fairfax.' The comparison was doubtless well intentioned — for Fairfax, before his switch to League at the age of twenty-two, had also been known for silken running and opportunism, for his ability to convert a 'half chance into a try in a twinkling'.[20]

Campese was already the 'most talked about player' in the competition. That led also to his selection for a training camp run by former Wallaby fullback Arthur McGill and national coaching director Dick Marks at the Holsworthy army barracks in Sydney. Six players from each state had been selected in what Campese called a 'poor man's Australian Institute of Sport', a clinic where they were taught more about how to 'swerve, kick, and tackle'. At the end of the camp, he recalls, each of the players was sat down and asked to articulate their goals. Campese's abrupt answer carried more than enough ambition: 'I said only six words: "I want to play for Australia."'[21]

Such was the 'talent, flair and confidence of this young colt that he is able to produce an advantage, and points from situations in which few others could'.[22] Campese, too, wanted to squeeze every last opportunity from the time left on the clock, such that you get the feeling that had each match had a third period, he would have been just as eager to play on. In one game, even as his side looked set for a comfortable, if close, victory over Dickson — the score being 17–15, with the final whistle imminent — Campese was depicted as having 'other ideas'. He 'fielded a clearing kick on the halfway, beat one tackle and then threaded his way through most of the Dickson side without being touched to score a brilliant solo try under the posts.'[23] By mid-July, Campese was already becoming a fixture in his own right:

> Like all who display youthful ability he has been praised and the pressure on him to perform increases with each match. Campese has not flinched and his care-free attitude off the field has helped him to maintain perspective about his ability. It is worth a trek to Manuka Oval to see the ACT Under-21s and Campese without worrying about the senior match.[24]

One can only wonder what the senior players thought of this kind of reporting — this was, after all, an occasion on which the Australian Capital Territory side was playing the touring All Blacks. It gave the none-too-subtle hint that, much like Bradman, the real action would be all over once Campese had left the field. But while the journalists came to praise, they also came to offer advice. At season's end, Campese's report card in the local press was favourable — he was 'one of the Whites' stars' — but the 'elimination of occasional errors' was the necessary precondition to his becoming 'the brilliantly classy player he so obviously is'.[25]

It was in 1981 that Campese started to break through more regularly into the representative sides, and it was during this season that the appellation of 'crowd pleaser' was first used. It was then, too, that rugby began to take him to the wider world, beyond Queanbeyan, in the form of a tour to New Zealand, and games at home, too, against touring French, Italian, and provincial sides from across the Tasman.

Campese was well and truly on his way now, but it was an occasionally bumpy ride. Playing in an Australian Capital Territory side that beat the reigning New Zealand champions, Waikato, Campese's 'magic was added to the game' with a 'grubber kick ... gathered in by the glue hands of the dashing David'.[26] The local press were hurt, however, perhaps more than Campese himself, when, for a subsequent match, their star was dropped to the reserves bench. As 'one wit remarked', said the *Queanbeyan Age*, 'Campese could walk on water and the selectors would still question his ability'.[27]

Due recognition was to come — in the form of selection for the Australian Under-21 side, and, later, a prized invitation as the youngest player ever to try out for the senior Australian team. This development revealed once more the Queanbeyan chip on the shoulder, the *Queanbeyan Age* noting with some relish that 'ironically [Campese] has received more recognition from the Australian selection panels than [from] the ACT selectors'. The right people, they meant — by implication, those with a national, not limited territorian, perspective — knew just what their local boy could do:

> His first tour with the ACT seniors was not the happiest one with the Canberra officials feeling that Campese must be suspect in some aspects of play because he was too good in other aspects. The Australian Under-21 officials were more confident of his ability and he was rewarded with more games and more scope to exercise his talents.[28]

Campese went on to give a 'good account of himself' in that Wallaby trial, scoring a 'fine try when he fielded a high ball and stepped around the defence'.[29] By year's end, he was touching down for a crucial four-pointer in the Whites' first grand final win since 1959. Running wide of all the cover defence, he took a long 20-metre spiral pass from his halfback, Mark Berry, and 'sprinted 25 metres diagonally to score'.[30]

The 'Struggletown shuffle'

That sense of local pride in Campese's achievements was to be given perhaps its fullest expression with the advent of the so-called Struggletown shuffle — the name given to Campese's trademark goosestep. The epithet 'Struggletown' arose in the 1950s because of the local council's preparedness to adjust building regulations in Queanbeyan to 'allow new settlers to live in temporary structures on their land while they were building their homes'. The proliferation of these sometimes-ramshackle dwellings, along with the garages and outhouses dotting the paddocks, fed the image of Queanbeyan as something of a poverty-stricken eyesore. Few labels drew as much ire from Queanbeyan residents, but it could equally be turned around, morphing into a grudging respect for the 'battlers' across the Australian Capital Territory border in New South Wales.[31]

Seen in this light, Campese's dancing feet showed the capacity of both the individual and the club to define local identity. This was all about advancement, if not literally on the field, in confounding an opponent from the capital, but by showing just what a kid from the sticks could achieve. The 'daring of Campese' described in the *Queanbeyan Age* sports pages had the habit of leaving 'defenders stretching at nothing', since he 'stepped around' them 'with his now famous Struggletown shuffle'. There was no way he was going to get hurt, said another, since 'they could not catch him'.

The fame of the move had come quickly, but it also brought with it a dose of reality. At the beginning of 1982, journalists pointed out that it was one thing to be 'the name on everyone's lips' in the local rugby scene, but quite another to get the national call-up: there was a 'long way between being talked about and making the Wallaby squad'.[32] None of this dampened Campese's cheekiness on the field, or the swelling numbers of people coming to see him play.

In some of the amateur footage from that season, a commentator — presumably a club member — can be heard exclaiming 'Campese, run easy, score-try easy!' It was hardly the suave tones of a Gordon Bray or the gravelly ebullience of a Norman May, but it got the point across: 'Where else would you go to see a try like that?' the voice bellowed. [33] In those grainy video clips, rows and rows of cars can be seen behind makeshift grandstands and fans hugging the sideline in various states of excitement. Queanbeyan club officials at the 'Mighty Whites' were having to bring in extra, even if temporary, grandstand seating for their home ground, Taylor Park, to accommodate the growing crowds attending their matches. They were coming to 'see Campese'.[34]

In Sydney, too, the Queanbeyan flyer had 'everyone standing up to take notice' and spectators 'rattling the grandstands' when, during a game against the New South Wales Under-21 side, he appeared to 'touch the ball down in his own in-goal area', a move that under the laws of the game would normally bring about a restart. But 'Mr Magic' had other ideas, and 'just bent down, feinted the touch and walked coolly down to the 22-metre line'. Then 'he took off, to the surprise of the NSW team', making considerable ground upfield 'in a move that exemplified his flair, cool and brilliance'.[35]

That desperate search for more grandstand space — they had to recycle old seating from Rugby Park in

Ainslie — came after Campese had won selection on the Wallaby tour of New Zealand for September. By this time, the sub-editors were really having a field day — the kid from Atkinson Street had used his 'Struggletown shuffle' to make the 'big hop' to being a Wallaby. Campese's selection came about as a result of a number of factors — especially his performances for the Australian Under-21 side against Fiji and New Zealand. A particular moment in one of these matches has been readily spliced into the tale of his rise to the top. It happened when Campese scored a try against the New Zealand Under-21 team at the Sydney Cricket Ground before the second Australia v Scotland international that year. Alan Jones remembers watching this young player 'virtually running on his toes' and saying to former Wallaby Terry Curley, who was standing alongside him, 'Who the hell is that?' Jones then dashed to find a program to discover the name. 'I just spelt it out rather quickly,' he recalls, 'C ... A ... M ... P ... E ... S ... E'.[36]

The rugby writer Spiro Zavos asserts he has now met thousands of people who claim to have been at the ground that day to witness the Campese performance. This, too, says much about the ease with which Campese was incorporated into a rather well-worn connection between fan and sporting idol: for to have been there when the hero first comes to national attention is to stake a special purchase on his discovery. Zavos's own description is itself noteworthy, if for no other reason than for his blending of alpine and battlefield descriptors. He recalls the young player stepping through the New Zealand defences 'like a slalom racer', leaving a number of his black-shirted opponents strewn in his wake, lying on the ground 'as if they'd been shot'.[37]

Campese's selection in the Wallaby touring team the day after that match was also partly related to another group of players stepping down — this time, in the form of a senior group of Wallabies who, on the eve of the team's announcement, declared themselves unavailable for selection.

Many books and newspaper articles have since attempted to draw out the reasons for this move, and opinion remains divided. Some see it as a snub, primarily from players north of the Tweed who harboured grievances against the Australian coach, Bob Dwyer, a New South Welshman. Some weeks before, Dwyer had aroused the ire of Queenslanders by dropping their favourite sons, Roger Gould and Paul McLean, in favour of Indigenous players Mark and Glen Ella for the first Test against Scotland in Brisbane. That decision led to perhaps one of the ugliest moments in Australian sporting history: a Queensland crowd booing an Australian side as it ran out to play a Test match. Campese has confessed to his shock, while sitting in the grandstand that day, at the way the national side was welcomed onto the field.

Others explain the mass player walkout as being on account of physical fatigue and financial stress: the prospect of another long, three-Test tour of New Zealand was unpalatable for some after what had been a lengthy domestic international season, coming on top of a nearly three-month tour of the British Isles in 1981–82. To be away for another two months was simply unworkable from the perspective of players who, after all, were still amateur.

But whatever the reason, Campese's inclusion in the Australian team once more saw the Queanbeyan club and community embrace him. That much is clear from the reporting of an emotional farewell that took place at the local rugby club on the eve of his departure for New Zealand. This was an event that contained its own set of rituals for the newly minted Australian player. Photos taken with his entire family, and with the coaches who had played a role in his career to date, were followed by a presentation of his representative Under-21 jersey for mounting on the clubhouse wall. Players and supporters supplied quotes to local journalists, emphasising that they were 'proud of the achievements of dashing David', while the committee members of the Australian Capital Territory Rugby Union, perhaps sheepish at having dropped him to the reserves the year before, 'congratulated themselves on producing another Wallaby'.

Campese's parents received special praise for 'bringing up a joey', while, in an act of what can only be described as a generous, if pitying, form of commemoration for the sporting fallen, special mention was made of 'the success of nameless others who have been on the brink but never quite made it'. Above all else, it seemed that the gathering revelled in Campese's success, for it was written that the 'Queanbeyan men ... bathed in the glory bestowed on a favourite'.[38]

'Just give it to that guy'

Campese's success on his first tour to New Zealand is now well documented — the concerns that its 'heavy grounds … may not suit his style' proved unfounded. Mouths were simply agape among the All Blacks and the Kiwi journalists at his speed and swerve — not to mention the 'unusual goosestep', which by now had been transformed into a 'trademark of his game when he wants to keep the opposition guessing', or a 'Muhammad Ali double shuffle, thank you', in the words of commentator Gordon Bray.[39]

At the start of the tour, in his first game in an Australian jersey against Manuwatu, the local coach labelled Campese a 'likely lad', while reports back in Australia stressed his 'high stepping action and blistering acceleration' that left the Manuwatu defence 'non-plussed'. The completion of what the *Canberra Times* called a 'dream debut' occurred as no player 'got within metres of Campese when he burst onto a pass from Mark Ella … [and] streaked 55 metres to touch down'.[40]

By the end of the tour, on the eve of an improbable decider at Eden Park, the esteemed New Zealand rugby writer TP McLean was praising these 'wonderful … inspiring' Wallabies for their success following the withdrawal of so many players before the tour — Campese being singled out 'for that leg action [which] could win the Commonwealth 110m hurdles in footie boots'.[41] Back in Queanbeyan, the locals felt that his All Black opponent, Stu Wilson, 'must see Campese coming at him in his sleep'.[42] Another All Black great, Grant Batty, lent further voice to the growing chorus of praise:

For a 19 year old he has shown remarkable confidence to take on a winger of the calibre of Stu Wilson the way he did ... And he has showed him a thing or two ... It's that little touch of uniqueness that makes him something special ... and there appears to be that touch of arrogance about his game that all great players have.[43]

This first tour of New Zealand was special for another reason: Campese played with the Ella brothers for the first time. All three brothers — the twins, Mark and Glen, and their brother, Gary, had been selected, and all of them played with Campese in that second game of the tour against Manuwatu. What resulted was not so much telepathy between the Ellas and Campese, as the recognition among the trio that in Campese they had what Mark called a 'kindred spirit' — someone else who simply wanted to 'keep the ball alive and to run with it'. Writing some years later, Mark remembered the nineteen-year-old Campese as 'very shy ... just a boy from the bush, really, and very raw', who 'didn't smoke, didn't drink and didn't socialise. All he was interested in was his sport.' That, Ella saw subsequently, was the essence of the Campese difference: that intensity, that striving for perfection, and the obsession with self-improvement. He was not, however, Ella added, 'shy on the field' in terms of showing his skills. What Ella was referring to was Campese's almost eerie ability to not be overawed by the occasion — the quietness came not from nerves, but from the confidence he'd been building over the previous decade. When, from his vantage point as the Australian five-eighth, he saw Campese step around Stu Wilson during that first Test in Christchurch, Ella knew that 'someone really special had come on the scene':

> Until then, much of Australia's attacking play had revolved around me. I was the one people looked to to initiate the moves, to set up the tries. Suddenly we had this young player on the wing, an absolute freak, who could do it all on his own. You could give him the ball with five players in front of him and he could either sidestep the lot of them or chip over the top, regather and score the try.[44]

Little wonder, then, that Campese was 'soon seen as an extension of the Ellas', or, as Mark later put it: he became the 'fourth Ella'. Mark summed it up neatly: he told his brothers to 'just give the ball to that guy'.[45]

There are hints, too, in these recollections of some frustration among teammates at Campese's evolving style of play. A sympathetic reading is that the young gun was a victim of his own unpredictability — if he claimed that he himself didn't know was coming next, how on earth could his teammates? The less-generous interpretation is that he was playing for himself alone. Some in the side, Ella remarked, found Campese 'impossible to read ... so unpredictable that nobody knew which angle to support'. That could lead to vituperative exchanges in the dressing rooms afterwards, particularly from players such as breakaway Simon Poidevin, who, like all backrowers, preferred their backs to run the standard angles they knew. 'Why don't you do what you're told and stick to the moves?' Poidevin supposedly once snapped at Campese after a match, because, he said, 'nobody can follow you'.[46] Roger Gould says, 'You'd get lost if you tried to track him. So the only way to follow Campese was to do so from 10 metres behind, so that when he 'unloaded the ball into the ether a teammate had a better chance of gathering the pass'.[47] Ella, too, conceded that Campese was 'impossible to follow', but he and his brothers worked out a system, in a way that sounds today as if they applied some kind of homing device to the young winger. The trick was not to simply follow him, but to look ahead, to translate not what was happening, but what was about to happen:

> My brothers and I ... were able to read Campese and more often than not were able to anticipate him. When Campese took off, we might see that he had, say, two immediate options, but that in either case he would have to come right eventually. So we would head to the right — in other words, take the short cut and meet him in the middle of the field.[48]

It hardly needs spelling out that the combination of the game's most famous Indigenous players with the son of an Italian migrant forged a unique relationship in the Australian game, but it is one that, surprisingly, has rarely been explored in any depth. Campese told author Bret Harris that he simply 'wanted to be like them'. Together, he added, 'we put ourselves out there'.[49] But the point is, too, that the regeneration of Australian rugby in this era was spearheaded by players who had been cultivated outside the private school nurseries.

No more goose

That sense of Campese's style being lost in translation might partially explain why, early the following season, he was publicly distancing himself from the very move that had won him early fame. By 1983, it seemed, the goosestep was in a state of transition, changing from an act of audacity to a commonplace occurrence, a move expected every time he took the field. It was becoming something akin to a magician's repetition of the same old card trick, or a rock star being asked to play an original hit tune yet one more time. The fatigue with it came not from spectators, who begged for more, but from Campese himself. He did not want to lose the element of surprise. To avoid the risk of it being overdone, it was to be put on stricter rations; indeed, as he told one newspaper, he wanted to 'wring the goose's neck'.

He 'couldn't get rid of it because it comes naturally ... but really, it's getting to be a bit of a pain. I used it far too much in New Zealand and it got to be obvious. The opposition was waiting for me to do it ... now everybody expects it all the time.' This led to a resolve — which lasted barely a couple of months — that he would hardly use it in future. It was not to be shelved entirely from the repertoire, however: 'I might do one if I get into trouble, but from now on, I'll be concentrating more on passing the ball and backing up rather than trying to make the breaks.'

It's tempting to conclude that the very harnesses that had not been slipped on in Queanbeyan were now being introduced: for these were the words of a responsible team player. But the words were redundant the moment they'd been uttered. In the same breath, he again expressed his desire to play fullback for Australia: the position he continued to play at club level. Already, Campese was letting it be known that it was 'pretty boring on the wing because you aren't involved in the game enough'. A 'fullback can do whatever he likes — the range of options are much greater'.[50]

Doing 'whatever he likes' — at the time, these were the kind of comments that might have sent a shiver down the spine of teammates, but they go to the heart of the Campese paradox, and they stand perhaps as the most apt summation of his early years in rugby. Few could dispute that he created space and opportunities for those he played alongside — the record and the minuting of each of his plays shows it — but there was from the very start of his playing career an unshakeable, instinctive individualism always straining at convention, and, very often, bursting through into space; at other times, bumbling into error.

Try as he might, Campese could not suppress these instincts. By early 1984 he was telling another journalist that 'you have to experiment, you have to do something different ... these days you have to invent new things and try the unusual like running the ball from your own line. Ten years ago you would never do that.'[51] Campese, though, had been doing it since his days in the Queanbeyan Under-10s.

When he looked up with the ball in his hand, he saw not obstacles in the form of defending players, but channels and paths through or around them. Space on a field was there to be used, diced, cut through on the way to the other side — and to that precious moment when he was untouched, unimpeded, and letting go. All by himself. Just running.

It is telling that towards the very end of his international career, in 1996, when, from Test match to Test match, Campese could not be sure of his position in the starting team, and as the sport was being catapulted into the professional era, the new Wallaby coach, Greg Smith, encouraged Campese to continue playing his normal game. There had been no diminution of Campese's desire to perform, of his excitement at being part of the 'code's new world' and of his conviction that the 'self-belief outweighed the self-doubts'. Rugby was 'still enjoyable': he had no trouble admitting he was 'clinging to it'. He also knew, however, that his powers were fading. The breathless acceleration had gone, and he had become more conservative. And he knew others knew. Smith, however, charted a different channel for him. As Campese remembers it, Smith told him 'to go out and play as if I was 19 years old again — to think back and remember how carefree I had played the game when still a teenager and representing the Wallabies for the first time in 1982 … I should treat every game as if I was at the start of my rugby days.'[52]

There is, of course, both a poignancy and pathos to this kind of advice being given to a sporting legend at the end of their career. It's the message, surely, that every veteran wants to hear: that they still have it, still retain that special touch of distinctiveness that sets them apart from all the others. Smith knew that it was impossible for Campese to recapture his form of the early 1980s at Taylor Park in Queanbeyan or at Lancaster Park in Christchurch, but he'd found a way to once more ignite Campese's approach to the game — a way, too, of connecting with the very essence of what made Campese the type of player he was.

In his defence of poetry, Percy Shelley disputed the suggestion that its composition could simply be the result of a blunt, declaratory act. One cannot simply say, he wrote:

'I will compose poetry.' The greatest poet even cannot say it; for the mind in creation is as a fading coal, which some invisible influence, like an inconstant wind, awakens to transitory brightness; this power arises from within.[53]

Something of this metaphysic might be said to have occurred in the making of David Campese. His creative acts on the field could be seen as moments of illumination for himself and for those around him — a realisation that he had to seize his talent, shape it, and develop it to the full before it faded. Campese has often said that when he was playing he remained unaware of which way his legs would take him. This suggests that the free spirit conditioned by his childhood and his natural talent — gifts allowed to develop without serious rupture or constraint in his path to adulthood — simply took over when he ran with the ball. It was instinct, not instruction, that drove him. But rugby was never just a game for Campese: his on-field performances were occasions for a special character to demonstrate not only his freedom to roam, but a speed that took him through and beyond the spaces that others could not see. And by the time they saw what he had already seen, it was too late. Campese was gone.

CHAPTER THREE

ACCLAIM

David Campese was interviewed in Italy by the *Sunday Times* in early 1989, and the photograph accompanying the article featured him clad in a dinner suit, standing before the gothic splendour of Milan Cathedral. His arms were outstretched, gesturing as if on stage in the midst of an operatic aria. The image played directly into the portrayal of Campese as both artist and performer; here, the Australian of Italian descent was once more plying his sporting trade on his father's ancestral lands. Like no other player of his generation, save perhaps for Frenchman Serge Blanco, Campese was often depicted more as an artist than an athlete, a description which in itself reflects an appreciation of the singularity of his playing style.

But this art had a shelf-life, and so came the inevitable question about when the final curtain might come down on his playing days. Asked about life after rugby, Campese evaded the question. 'Deep inside,' he said, 'I just want this to go on forever.'[1] He was anticipating what all who reach the top fear — not being there anymore, and, moreover, what normality brings. At that point in his career, it was not hard to see why Campese was giving expression to this sentiment. Just months before, he had achieved a rarity for international rugby players: a standing ovation on a foreign field. And in this case it came from the Welsh crowd at Cardiff Arms Park — not the kind of fans to bestow that kind of honour lightly.

The moment came in the final match of the Wallabies' 1988 tour of the United Kingdom, a fixture against the Barbarians. Such matches have long provided the finale for visiting touring teams in this part of the world, where the inhibitions of Test rugby are cast aside, and entertainment — for that, read running the ball from everywhere — is the order of the day. This particular game had been given a special edge by the local and visiting press, since the Barbarians' line-up featured many of the players from the four countries — England, Ireland, Scotland, and Wales — who would in the following year comprise the bulk of the British and Irish Lions side to tour Australia. Barbarians games have produced some of the most scintillating tries in rugby history. The most replayed — even today — remains Gareth Edwards' score following a breathless, at times almost improbable, series of passes from one end of the field to the other against the All Blacks at Cardiff in 1973.

Towards the end of this match in 1988, Campese scored a try that has been described as one of his finest. Taking the ball on the halfway line, he sped, dodged, weaved, dummied, and scorched his way to the line in a dazzling, mesmerising run that had some players beaten for sheer pace, others left stationary by his swerve, and still more clutching at nothing in the wake of his sidesteps off both feet. Welsh writer Alun Richards once described the young Welsh player Carwyn James as 'sidestepping on his enemy's shadow, dancing away, playing torero with his heels until his pursuer finally fell sprawling, hands grasping the air'.[2] Now Campese was following in James's footsteps. The doyen of rugby television commentators, the Scotsman Bill McLaren, described Campese's try as 'sheer genius from the moment he touched the ball'.[3] Writing in the *Guardian* some years later, Frank Keating called it 'daringly opulent'; in the *Times* around the time of the Rugby World Cup in 1991, Stephen Jones remembered it as 'searing'.[4] Before Campese's exploits at that tournament, it was this try that was the showcase of all the gifts he brought to the game.

After the try, Campese's teammates joined the crowd, clapping him all the way back to the halfway line — the winger wearing a sheepish grin until he, too, began to applaud, if only because he felt it was the right thing to do, and because he wanted to acknowledge the teammates who had delivered him the kind of possession that made the try possible. As Bill McLaren gushed on air, 'The whole of Cardiff Arms Park rises to this genius.' The standing ovation was only the second time a Welsh crowd had stood for someone not of their own — the other occasion being for New Zealand prop forward and captain Wilson

Whineray, in 1964, when the grandstands had burst into a rendition of 'For He's a Jolly Good Fellow'. Australian journalists at the ground saw the applause for Campese as akin to a confirmation of the sacred: some, more tongue-in-cheek than others. Four spectators ran on to the ground at the end of the game bearing a sign saying 'Dave Campese walks on water'. The *Australian*'s Greg Campbell contended that if 'Cardiff Arms Park is the cathedral of rugby', Campese had just been 'ordained as its Archbishop'. The *Sydney Morning Herald*'s sub-editors reached for the Bible: under the headline 'King David tames the Barbarians', its correspondent Greg Growden described the fans leaving their seats to 'make the Campese tribute echo to almost thunderous proportions'.[5]

But the most powerful description of the crowd reaction appeared in a Cardiff newspaper the morning after the match, when the former Welsh and British Lions winger Gerald Davies found the words to match the occasion:

> At this crowning moment the crowd hailed the conquering hero and gave him the accolade of a standing ovation. For as he sauntered behind the posts, they saw in him what they had seen all along but were too reluctant to admit: the rugby player they themselves would wish to be.[6]

Campese later said that he'd kept Davies' article in his wallet for years afterwards: his own way, perhaps, of trying to hold on to the ovation, to freeze it in time, even if only in print. While his other clippings were routinely sent home to his mother, this one remained with him. 'Well, it *was* Gerald Davies,' Campese admitted. This was, of course, one international winger basking in the praise of one of his most esteemed predecessors in that position. If, as Welsh poet Owen Sheers has written, his compatriots demand 'a style of play, a philosophy, inherited from that Welsh rugby past: inventive and audacious, physical yet graceful', then Campese had fitted the bill. The sustained clapping said he was one of them.[7]

Gerald Davies had captured the essential, emotional current that flowed between spectator and player whenever Campese played. Spectators wanted to be like him. Stephen Jones likewise sensed this when he wrote that Campese was a 'man in love with theatre and audience and sensation'. To watch Campese on these brilliant occasions was not only to experience something beyond the everyday; it was to witness the outer limits of what was possible on a rugby field. Teresa Lancerd and Stephen Mumford have argued that 'watching an athlete freely in control of their abilities provides a beautiful experience for the spectator because it can be seemingly effortless and gracious'.

Theoretically, there was simply no way that one player should have been able to score such a try, one which combined all his mercurial skills in an outrageous demonstration of physical movement: his reading of the play and anticipation of where the gaps would appear; his mesmerising change of pace; and his ability to confound and deceive his opponents — all without losing speed or balance.

He was, in this moment, akin to David Foster Wallace's description of tennis great Roger Federer, a 'creature whose body is both flesh and, somehow, light'.[8]

After a lifetime of watching and writing about the sport, Spiro Zavos has argued that rugby is watched 'tribally, aesthetically, intellectually and fantastically'. And watching Campese, admitted one diehard fan to Zavos, was 'always pure pleasure'. For the New Zealand author Maurice Gee, there is 'something almost beautiful in rugby when it is played properly. You can see the patterns and the movements and you almost appreciate it aesthetically.'[9] But perhaps its most complete expression came from Carwyn James, who, following the briefest of international careers, went on to coach the successful 1971 British Lions team in New Zealand. James said that he saw 'rugby football as a piece of opera, a piece of music. It is something that can flow like music and opera and can be beautiful to watch.'[10] The scratchy, discordant moments that rugby, if not all sports, inevitably contains were obliterated when an individual or a team hit the right notes of unity and style.

This Welsh adulation of Campese illustrates his special appeal to rugby fans in the United Kingdom. British rugby journalist Mick Cleary believed Campese was 'the darling of the crowds' because he could 'transcend the petty boundaries of nationalism which are so evident at games these days'.[11] Stephen Jones, at the end of a Wallaby tour to England and Scotland in 1992, remarked of Campese that 'it is preposterous to believe rugby will ever again see a player like him. Such a rich adornment, such a draw for people who come to sport to sit up and be endlessly fascinated. Prepare now the mental fireside for Campese tales for your grandchildren.'[12] The *Sydney Morning Herald*'s Greg Growden filed a report during the 1992 Welsh tour: 'Here in Wales', he wrote, Campese had only to take a 'few hesitant steps out of the hotel' to 'prompt scenes almost reminiscent of the Beatles'.[13] It is not uncommon, of course, for players to be accorded some kind of legendary, mythical status even before they have retired. And Campese was more loved in Britain and elsewhere overseas than in his home country. But the point is Campese had to travel outside his own country to find the true appreciation he clearly craved. Not only was his play in Britain often superior to his performances in Australia, but his critics on the home front were harsher.

Explaining this affection has to involve much more than the British seeing in Campese a mixture of good old-fashioned colonial dash and daring, blended with an exotic splash of continental sophistication and elegance. Campese's answer to this question is far more straightforward: he says there was simply 'no pressure over there'. Everyone in Europe, he felt, was 'interested in what you could do and not in what you couldn't do, whereas in Australia there are an awful lot of people who seem to expect you to be doing something brilliant all the time. We all know it doesn't work like that.'[14] He felt that British crowds not only loved his sense of adventure, but that the occasional error or slip was built into the player–spectator bargain: the idiosyncratic dimension was accepted rather than spurned.

It might be said that in Britain, and indeed in France and Italy, Campese had found his Elysian fields: where the freedom to be himself came with ready forgiveness if things went awry. In terms of official plaudits, the relationship that Campese enjoyed with British rugby spectators and aficionados reached its high point following the 1991 World Cup, when the *Rothmans Rugby Union Yearbook* named him as one of its five players of the year. In its justification for the ranking, the editors claimed that Campese in that era 'became as famous as any British rugby player, or even any British sportsman', and for that reason 'he had to accept a succession of prestigious awards for the impact he made on the consciousness of British sport'.[15]

Greg Growden discerned a change in Campese's appearance, outlook, and general demeanour when playing in the Northern Hemisphere. Whereas in Australia Campese would 'unconsciously stoop' with his 'head down … shoulders slumped … eyes nervous, the mind looking for an exit, the demons after him', in Britain he strutted 'like a conqueror': 'the swagger returns, the chest is thrust out, the eyes are ablaze, the once hesitant footsteps become a prance, the voice and the mind again become obsessive, even cocky'. The demons were gone, dispatched.

The reason, Growden suggested, had much to do not only with Campese's desire for acceptance, but also with the feeling that in Britain and elsewhere in Europe he was 'cushioned by allies' — especially a tabloid press in London that adored him to the extent of being 'the unconscious leaders of the David Campese fan club'.[16] The British tabloids liked Campese's ability to provoke sensation off the field with his unguarded, blunt commentary, as much as it did his exploits on it. Even Campese's no-nonsense remarks to the press, his goading of English players in particular, and his unashamed playing of the Australian nationalist card when it suited him did little to dent his reputation in that part of the world.

But, without question, the majority of Campese's most brilliant moments — the ones for which he is most remembered — did occur on fields abroad, and particularly those in the British Isles. During tours there in 1984, 1988, 1992, and 1996, and of course as a member of the winning World Cup side of 1991, the British sporting public saw him and the Wallabies reveal a running game that was often praised for its artistry, style, creativity, and innovation. For some Australian journalists, not to mention rugby officials, the British applause was gratifying in its reflected glory. This acclaim — for the team at least — was very much sought out and gratefully received, and underlined the continuing need in the national imagination for sporting accomplishments to be achieved by Australian individuals and teams in Britain. It connected, as historian Graeme Davison pointed out, to a deep-seated anxiety about winning 'the good opinion of Mother England'.[17]

Winning such plaudits might appear to have been unnecessary to the Australia of the 1980s and early 1990s, which was supposed to have left the cultural cringe behind as it stepped out more confidently onto the world stage. But what is striking in Australian accounts of Wallaby successes in this era, particularly overseas, and especially victories won in Britain or Ireland, is just how much confirmation of this success — of Australian pre-eminence, no less — relied on British and Irish observers and journalists. They alone, it seems, had the right to confer rugby immortality. To reach the gateway to rugby heaven, an Australian team still had to journey through London, Dublin, Cardiff, and Edinburgh.

This Wallaby success in the 1980s addressed an eager Australian sporting public. The national psyche was barely recovering from the country's own relative sporting decline in the 1970s. At the 1976 Olympics, no Australian athlete had brought home a gold medal, a development that led to the creation of the Australian Institute of Sport — to ensure the embarrassment could never be repeated. Around the time that Campese was beginning to make his mark as a Wallaby, the country's cricketers were either being bludgeoned by a buccaneering Ian Botham wielding English willow or terrorised by the West Indian pace attack. In 1984, the Australian cricket captain, Kim Hughes, had tearfully resigned at a press conference during a Test match in Brisbane, stressed by the legacy of the cricket wars and by vitriolic criticism from the press and from current and former Australian cricketers.

There was some respite with the 1982 Rugby League 'Invincibles' tour of Britain, the 1983 America's Cup win, and gold-medal-winning performances at the 1984 Olympics. Australian cricket's winning ways had been restored by the end of the 1980s. But the success of the Wallabies in the United Kingdom and also in New Zealand in 1986, where they won a rare Bledisloe Cup series, has persuasive claims to have been the most significant Australian sporting achievements of the decade.

Grand Slam

The El Dorado for Australian rugby in the 1980s remained an unbeaten tour of the United Kingdom and Ireland. For all the unbridled joy that had come with victory over the All Blacks on home soil in 1980, the fact that so many previous Wallaby touring teams had come away from tours of the 'home Unions' without the coveted Grand Slam — meaning victory in the Test matches against England, Ireland, Scotland, and Wales — suggested that Australian rugby had not yet quite made it. The 'coming of age' rhetoric that accompanied a win over the All Blacks clearly had its limits. Until Australian teams conquered those four sides in one fell swoop, their claims to global rugby supremacy were deemed hollow. Never mind that in the preceding five years, Australian rugby teams had beaten — and convincingly, if at times thuggishly — English, Welsh, and Scottish teams in Sydney and Brisbane. But on the two most recent tours to the United Kingdom, in 1976 and 1981, any hope of confirming an Australian rugby renaissance had come to an end on the grounds of Twickenham, Cardiff Arms Park and Murrayfield.

This is not to say that the running game for which Australian teams were fast developing a reputation had in any way run aground on the lush turf of those hallowed stadia. Quite the contrary. The *Sunday Times'* respected rugby columnist Viv Jenkins had praised the 1976 Wallaby tourists for their 'uninhibited attacking running' that had shown up the 'stodgy, uninspired play of the home teams', praising them for 'carrying the torch for adventurous running rugby'.[18]

However, the 1981 tour was a particular letdown — a film crew and a poet, no less, had even accompanied the Australian team to make a documentary of its impending Grand Slam success, which was treated as a virtual certainty after the Bledisloe Cup triumph of the previous year. Expectations had risen, too, because, in between those two tours, an Australian schoolboys' team — featuring the Ella brothers, Michael O'Connor, Tony Melrose, Michael Hawker, and Wally Lewis — had gone through the United Kingdom on an unbeaten tour that had captivated the British press. In November 1981, the bible of British rugby, *Rugby World*, had even graced its front cover with a photo of fullback Roger Gould at full steam with the headline 'Wallabies aim for Grand Slam'. In a centrefold, readers were told to 'watch these Wallabies go'. Within, a profile of burly forward Mark Loane affirmed that 'victory in three or more of the four internationals would see these tourists hailed as the new champions of the rugby world'. In the past, it was noted, the Wallabies had been 'looked upon as rather a soft touch in the internationals. Not this time. Winning the Tests is the main reason they are here.'[19]

Alas, while that tradition of running rugby — and scoring tries with it — was clearly fulfilled by the 1981 side, poor goal-kicking by Paul McLean meant that they departed the British Isles with only one Test win from four matches.

Winning aside, the very fact that Britain and Ireland were still referred to as the 'home' Unions also says much about the pungent whiff of empire that still hung over the sport in this era. The idea of Britain as ancestral territory had been slowly disappearing from the Australian lexicon since the 1960s, though mass jumbo-jet air travel in the following decade had given more Australians than ever before the chance to visit the United Kingdom and see its sights, to see their parents' and grandparents' homelands.

The team's tour itinerary, too, still bore the rites and rituals from another age. The 1984 Wallabies were given a lavish welcome lunch at the Savoy — the preferred hotel lodgings of Australian prime ministers on visits to London — and on this occasion the event featured 'remarks' by former British prime minister Edward Heath and a toast to Her Majesty the Queen. A visit to the Queen herself at the Palace, too, was de rigueur, captain Andrew Slack telling one newspaper that while there was 'growing Republican flavour amongst Australians … everybody, even the anti-monarchists in the team, were impressed by the palace'.[20] Coach Alan Jones had done his very best to instil a sense of patriotism in the side by holding singing lessons as part of the preparation for the tour in St Andrews College Chapel at Sydney University — with 'Waltzing Matilda', 'Advance Australia Fair', and 'I Still Call Australia Home' among the repertoire. A three-month immersion in British and Irish culture, replete with visits to theatres in London, castles, and other historic locations such as Shakespeare's birthplace at Stratford-upon-Avon, can only have reinforced not only the British roots of the game itself, but also the old British world out of which their own country emerged.

Nineteen eighty-four would be David Campese's first-ever visit to the United Kingdom, and in his memoir he argued correctly that the 'trail the 1984 Wallabies blazed through Great Britain and Ireland created effects on the game in that part of the world which are still acknowledged today'. The 'shake up our success gave to British rugby' meant it was 'the most influential tour I have ever been on'.[21] Campese's attacking flair and the threat it posed was being discussed in intriguing ways. Writing nearly a year before the team arrived in Britain, journalist Alex Wilson remarked that 'just occasionally a little gem appears in life and Campese is a throwback to the attacking, breathtaking rugby of which we all yearn and probably delude ourselves as to its eventual return'. It was the first time that Campese had been written about, in depth, in the British rugby press. Moreover, Wilson made the point that the 'stereo-typed game which has all but engulfed most parts of the British Isles seems a poor substitute for the brand marketed by Campese and his colleagues'. Even at this point in his career, Campese was not holding back:

[T]he Lions, Wales, England ... all seem to base their play around the forwards. At best it is ten man rugby, with the first five eight being told to kick, with the forwards charging after it. I cannot see how a crowd gets really excited with that sort of rubbish. OK, it works, but personally, I like keeping the crowd happy and therefore keeping them coming back to rugby.

Here was an early glimpse of how the British rugby public was willing to accept criticism of their own game from a truly thrilling player. Wilson went for a distinctly British image to conclude his profile, that of a light appearing through the foggy gloom, as if Campese was a lone, lantern-bearing figure emerging from the darkness on a wintry English morning. He was like those 'carriers of beacons in olden times spreading the news'. Who, Wilson asked, 'can in total honesty place his hand upon heart and deny that the flair merchants like Campese bring a flutter of excitement to the rugby grounds of the world?'[22]

But it was Wallaby coach Alan Jones who delivered the most striking pre-tour description of Campese — one clearly designed to resonate with a British, as much as an Australian, audience. Jones had become coach of the Wallabies earlier in 1984, and a month before the Wallabies arrived in London to begin the tour, he told one journalist that 'our star wing, David Campese, is a great thinker and has the potential to be Australian rugby's Don Bradman'. The tag, which soon morphed into Campese being the 'Bradman of rugby', became something of both a crown and a curse for him. As Campese tells it, when he made mistakes on the field — as in New Zealand in 1986, when he threw a wild pass infield that led to a soft All Black try — Jones would apparently tell him he was not living up to the Bradman tag. But what is significant here is its deployment in the media immediately before an Australian sporting team set foot on British soil.

Campese's Bradman mantle was to take on a life of its own. No doubt, Jones was using the description to instil some kind of fear in British rugby minds — if Bradman was the run-scoring machine, Campese was his try-scoring equivalent. As Jones was to later say, the comparison was far more straightforward: just as the crowds wanted to see Bradman bat, so they wanted to see Campese with the ball. Certainly, too, the goosestep had been depicted before the tour less as artistry than as artillery. Journalist Barry Newcombe affirmed in the days before the team landed at Heathrow that Campese's goosestep was a 'weapon they are unleashing for the first time against the home countries'. Welsh centre Rob Ackerman, who had played against Campese in the Canberra competition some years before, presented first-hand evidence:

> He uses the goosestep to beat people. It's really confusing because he checks himself with it and then he goes off in another direction … I think he could cause a lot of damage.

Ackerman could not have known that he would be toyed with by Campese — to the point of almost sheer embarrassment — in the final match of the tour against the Barbarians in Cardiff. Wallaby captain Andrew Slack, perhaps not wanting to reveal too much of the weaponry his team was bringing, was more cagey than his coach. Campese, he said, 'can be devastating ... and he has these interesting evasive skills. It's not just a normal sidestep. It's a ... well, you'll see.'[23] Slack was clearly engaging in his own bit of pre-tour mental jousting — but it's also tempting to take some poetic licence and see him, even if not explicitly, putting the same kind of shroud over Campese's running as that which had covered Ben Lexcen's winged keel, the innovation that lay, quite literally, beneath *Australia II*'s successful 1983 America's Cup bid.

Putting aside the normal banter that precedes major sporting events, Alan Jones had a point: the resonance and power of the Bradman/Campese comparison did not come from the simple equation of tries to runs; rather, it was the effect that Campese had on the crowds, and especially on British crowds. Gideon Haigh contended that Bradman's first and last tours of England 'bracket ... his cricket career like the books of Genesis and Revelation'. By the time of his final tour there in 1948, the bond that had formed between British crowds and Bradman was complete: the English cricket writer RC Robertson-Glasgow appeared to speak for many when he observed that 'we want him to do well ... we feel we have a share in him. He is more than Australian. He is a world batsman.'[24]

This ties in to the points made by Mick Cleary, and later Stephen Jones, about the rarity of Campese's gifts enabling him to 'transcend nationalism'. After the Wallabies had completed their grand slam with a win by 37–12 over Scotland in Edinburgh (following wins by 19–3 over England in London, 16–9 over Ireland in Dublin, and 28–9 over Wales in Cardiff), Scottish journalist Norman Mair observed similarly that the 'rugby of the Wallabies transcended mere patriotism and left anyone with a real feeling for the game enchanted'. Mair, too, reached for Bradman:

> The crowd saluted them rather as they used to rise to Don Bradman after he had butchered the England attack. 'Poetry and murder lived in him together', said Somerset's Scotsman, RC Robertson-Glasgow, of the Don and so might we say of the Wallabies who took Scotland apart at Murrayfield.[25]

Although the 1984 tour is rightly remembered for being Mark Ella's genius-laden swansong to Australian rugby, his try in each of the four Tests being a feat never before — or since — achieved, there can be no doubt, too, that the same tour was the beginning of something akin to a special relationship between Campese and British crowds. Like Bradman, too, Campese would play his last Test for Australia on British soil, at Cardiff Arms Park, in 1996.

Art and adventure

These differences in British and Australian styles and approaches to the game expressed themselves in ways that clearly suggested much more was at stake than a mere result.

Verdicts about national character and identity were also being delivered. The Wallabies had given the English team at Twickenham a 'lesson in adventure', they had 'damaged Welsh morale' by scoring a pushover try in Cardiff, and had given the game across the entire British Isles the 'kiss of life'. As a result of the tour, one tabloid journalist begged British sportsmen to find some 'guts' and stop being 'riddled with fear', rattling off a list of recent sporting failures that had him stretching all the way back to Britain's World Cup soccer win in 1966 for some uplifting news. Incredulity was never far from this commentary. 'Why is it,' asked Alan Thomson, 'Australians can beat us at Rugby Union and at Rugby League [in 1982] with two of the great sides of modern times? They have no more players from whom to select.'[26] In its own way, this was as good as the sneer that Australian captain Tony Shaw had felt eight years earlier.

Reading through the match reports and analysis from that northern winter of 1984, it is impossible to escape the frequency with which British rugby commentators mentioned the way in which the Australian team used the full width of the rugby pitch: their open running and risk-taking along with the swift movement of the ball from one side to the other catching the eye. The *Daily Express*'s Tony Bodley hailed it as nothing less than a 'glorious celebration of the splendours of the game'. David Frost in the *Times* could only have been talking of Campese when he concluded that 'where the current Wallabies have brought innovation is in their use of the disengaged wing three-quarter as an extra centre ... Wallaby wings do not stay twiddling their thumbs while movements are being fashioned towards the other side of the field. They make sure they are in position to join in the attack with the aim of creating the overlap.'[27] Bill Beaumont, a former England captain, marvelled at the Australians 'moving the ball and creating space'.[28] And after the game at Murrayfield, the Scotland player John Rutherford confessed that British players were simply 'too set in our ways to change and it is up to schools to teach boys the Australian approach of close alignment and quick passing, which allows them to break the gain line early and create scoring openings'. The Australian backs, he noted 'were brought up as boys to play in this style'.

The question of art, technique — even music — was never far from the discussion, either, where this Australian team was concerned. Thus, at the end of the tour, Gerald Davies channelled cricket writer Neville Cardus to make the point that among the crowd in the stands it was not the technical jargon that mattered when watching a batsman play, but rather the overall effect, the 'completeness of the stroke'. From there, Davies' appreciation for what the 1984 side had pulled off is worth quoting in full:

> The art of any game is to conceal the artifice; not to give the game away by showing your intentions. The player's art, like the actor's art, should not reveal the energy and the thought, the sweat and the spit, and the theory that has gone on into rehearsal. Nor should the anxiety surface from beneath the skin. Come the performance it somehow should look easy and effortless. This may seem a

long way round to get to the Australians' game, but theirs has been made to seem easy and effortless. The observer is not aware of the detail of their game, only of the overall colourful impression.[29]

Davies was talking as if observing a masterpiece in a gallery, musing on the preparation and skill that had gone into the work, but trying not to think too hard about the detail of its making, for fear of missing what was supposed to be up for ultimate appreciation: the sweeping impression. But he was talking, too, about a 'British gallery seeking its lost art'. Davies was, in essence, wiping away nearly a generation of condescension in the British Isles towards Australian rugby, turning the cultural cringe on its head, for the 1984 Wallabies had given their hosts a lesson in the art of the game.

One rugby historian believed that the Wallaby backline, in particular, merited 'comparison with the great Welsh names of 1971', the year in which the Welsh side, boasting a backline comprising the likes of Gareth Edwards, Barry John, Gerald Davies, and JPR Williams — players who in Wales were treated as near-celestial beings — had won the Grand Slam.[30] For all their unique and individual talent, the Wallabies were, in some respects, a reminder for Welsh supporters of lost glories. Making a similar point to Davies', the *Sydney Morning Herald*'s Evan Whitton believed that the 1984 Wallabies epitomised 'JS Bach's Baroque stuff, in which an essential unity was achieved by a balance among diverse elements'.[31]

Light, too, was a constant metaphor in much of the commentary — as it had been in 1982 when Rugby League writers in the United Kingdom had drawn similar conclusions about the unbeaten Australian Kangaroos touring side.[32] In 1984, the word 'beacon' made a number of appearances, perhaps not surprisingly given the dazzling sight of fifteen gold jerseys running rings around home defences during a dark English winter. Eddie Butler, who was in the losing Welsh team, said later that the Wallaby side on that tour was 'at the cutting edge of all things to do with rugby':

> The collective mentality, the individual skills, the fitness levels, the man management off the field, the man management on the field, everybody knowing what they were doing ... they were just light years ahead of us ... it was a beacon of glory.[33]

Butler had been talking particularly about the capacity of the Australian side to attack from all corners of the field. In a similar vein, the *Mail on Sunday*'s John Taylor remarked that the Wallabies' 'wit and flair shone out like a beacon on wet and dismal Murrayfield', and the *Daily Telegraph*'s John Mason discerned 'amid the damp, sepulchral gloom of Murrayfield, a beacon-like message [that] penetrated every corner'.[34] Bill McLaren barely baulked at making the claim that the Australian team 'revolutionised international rugby', but 'certainly they produced a form of back play that was so challenging and so exciting that people were really taken aback by the sheer quality of it'.[35] All of this was exultant. And on the basis of these bouquets being thrown the Australians' way, the conclusions reached by one of Australia's chief rugby correspondents at the time, Terry Smith, could leave no doubt: 'Australian rugby had finally made it.' This, mind you, was a mere four years after the sport's first 'coming of age', in the 1980 series against New Zealand.

Perhaps the only slightly less effusive note was struck by Stephen Jones, correspondent for the London *Times*. At the end of the tour, Jones wrote that while there could be no doubt that the Australians 'were virtuosi', there was good reason to hold back from the 'starry-eyed euphoria' that had laced the press appraisals of the Wallabies that week. British rugby, Jones claimed, was in a state of near total disarray, with England and Ireland recovering from a period of 'collapse', the Welsh 'dreadful', and the Scots, who had won the Five Nations championship the year before, simply 'unrecognisable'. The 'combined efforts of the four international teams ranged against [Australia] never amounted to more than a rabble'. Sure, he confessed, Australia won a Grand Slam, but 'so in the prevailing circumstances would Romania, Cardiff, Pontypool, the second XVs of South Africa, and New Zealand. Old Rottinghamians would have stood a chance, too.'[36]

Jones' conclusions were cutting, but they heralded what came to be the accepted wisdom about 1984. The most eminent Australian rugby historian Jack Pollard concluded that 'the opposition the eighth Wallabies faced was disappointing and it would be a mistake to label this the greatest Australian side. Overall the Wallabies encountered teams either weakened by injuries or in the rebuilding phase. They were never tested.' Luck, too, played its part, one of the driest northern winters meaning that 'they seldom had to slither around in the mud'.[37] Campese himself wrote, too, that while he did not wish to 'diminish our achievement', he had to 'be honest and say that I don't think the standard of British and Irish rugby was crash-hot at the time'. All the flair of some of the great names of the sport there — Gareth Edwards, David Duckham, JPR Williams, and Tony Ward — 'seemed to have been lost to the British game'.[38]

Unrequited love

But this was Campese at his most diplomatic. Indeed, for all the affection directed his way in Britain, it was rarely returned, especially during his playing days. Campese seemed to go out of his way to provoke a reaction from the press, supporters, and players whenever he appeared in the British Isles. There was seemingly no boat he did not seek to rock; no one's pride he did not wish to injure, or, at times, insult. When Campese spoke of the need to remember that 'when you go on tour you are representing your country' and of the need to establish a 'good reputation on and off the field', he was clearly taking aim at the boorish, oafish, and alcohol-fuelled behaviour that can sometimes be the hallmark of overseas tours. Campese, as he had done since his earliest playing days in Queanbeyan, stood at a clear distance from that culture. But such nods to protocol and responsibility clearly never extended to a level of ambassadorial finesse when it came to talking about his opponents or their playing styles.

Indeed, Campese came to resemble a diplomat speaking off the record, but then deciding to leak the transcripts of private discussions to passing journalists. Those journalists, of course, were just as eager to pluck a juicy quote from the loquacious Australian. Campese's memoir is replete with his unvarnished commentary on British teams: Scottish sides were 'dull' and 'limited'; the Welsh suffered from a 'lack of pride in their national team' — no comment could be more calculated to offend a Welsh supporter, even if in that era it might have been true; and Five Nations rugby was 'boring'. Only Ireland seemed to escape relatively unscathed, since, with his anthropological hat on, Campese came to the judgement that Irish people didn't have an 'in-built arrogance about them', like the Welsh.[39] England centre Jeremy Guscott had to 'learn to think not only for himself and what he can achieve', and the 'word in the game is that he may be worried about taking the hard knocks'.

England captain Will Carling came in for special attention, particularly in the week before the World Cup final in 1991, when Campese taunted him for being a 'typical upper class English public school chap, the bloke born with the silver spoon in his mouth'. That comment could have come all the way from Atkinson Street in Queanbeyan, the public school drop-out giving two rhetorical fingers to the suave playboy of the British rugby establishment. For good measure, Campese said that 'we wanted to stuff Will Carling'. The entire England team was taken to task for its lack of ability in playing attacking, running rugby. Out came the nationalist card, too, when he said that Australia would prevail, since his opponents were a 'bunch of toffs and we are convicts'. 'Beating the Poms', he added, was about triumphing over the 'blokes who represent the old country'.[40] This tactic, it must be said, seemed to work, for England in that final did ditch their more traditional forwards-oriented game, and ran the ball at the Australians from everywhere, without success. Campese, for years, twisted the knife into that 1991 England side by pointing out that since they didn't come from a tradition of running rugby, they were unable to flick a switch to do so for just that match.

Campese seemed to relish the self-appellation of 'stirrer'. And clearly this was little more than a fairly traditional, if not downright predictable, tradition of 'Pommie-bashing'. Some, such as Bill McLaren, were prone to waving it breezily away — either by saying that Campese was a 'cheeky chappie who would speak his mind' or that his comments on English rugby 'went down very well with the Celtic countries, especially Scotland and Ireland.' Others, such as the former England second rower Paul Ackford, said that Campese's off-field commentary should be taken with 'half a ton of salt', since the real Campese was quiet, self-effacing, and even shy.[41]

Still others, though, were not quite so willing to forgive and forget. In 2003, after England had won the World Cup final in Australia, Campese made good on a pre-game promise to walk around London bearing a sandwich board declaring that 'I admit the best team won'. But when he was subsequently asked by the BBC to present the award for 'Team of the Year' to the triumphant England team, its coach Clive Woodward was not impressed: 'to pick a guy that has little or no respect in the world of international rugby was a crass decision', Woodward seethed. And he, too, was the very kind of individual who epitomised the British rugby type that Campese despised. But not all agreed: the show's editor countered that Campese 'has had to eat humble pie, and we thought that would embellish the strength of England's achievement', while one of the England players, Josh Lewsey, clearly bought into the gag, adding that 'it was amazingly satisfying to have Campese, of all people, present us with the award'.[42]

But Campese's willingness to criticise all things British changed. This speaks to something else in terms of his attitude to rugby tradition. Initially, at least, he may not have wished to show due deference to the sites and symbols of British rugby. He may not have wanted to reveal his own susceptibility to what the game in the Northern Hemisphere offered in terms of its historic habits and customs, deriving as they did from a background that was in many ways alien to that which had surrounded him back home. Most likely he didn't want to demonstrate quite so openly just how he, too, over the life of his career, had come to be taken in by the particular culture that enveloped the game in that part of the world. In a remarkably frank assessment of his early impressions of stadiums in the British Isles, there is almost a concerted attempt to show that he was unaffected by this aura, that he was aloof to all the emotion poured into the British rugby atmosphere:

> I scoffed at the so-called mysticism of Cardiff and that was my sincere belief. For me, all these supposed shrines … are all just patches of grass. I found it strange that people talked about such places with so much awe. At least that was my first impression on my initial visit to these grounds. But having played there a few times since, I now realise that without the great tradition of such grounds, rugby in Britain would not mean as much as it does.[43]

He could have been describing Taylor Park just down the road from his childhood home. But by the time of his last Test match for Australia, fittingly played in Cardiff, the transformation was truly complete. Campese was even more effusive, saying that 'every time I have played at [this] ground has been a great experience, and obviously I have really appreciated being part of some marvellous matches on such a famous and great oval'. Moreover, he had 'always enjoyed playing in front of Welsh crowds. They seem to appreciate me, which is great.'[44] It would have not surprised had Campese gone on to agree with the Welsh writer David Tossel that among the 'passionate congregation in the Cardiff Arms Park — even the name had its own captivating rhythm' was where Campese felt most at home in the rugby world. However much he wanted to remain the

Queanbeyan kid untouched by the weight of history and heritage, in the end it, too, engulfed him, even charmed him, and made him one of its own.

Of course, it was in Campese's interests — in terms of his legacy alone — to allow this to happen. Many in Britain were not only happy to ignore his frequent, if cheap, provocations, but they were also willing to tend the flame of his memory in a way that differed from the reception he was sometimes afforded in Australia. So it is hardly surprising that Campese would come to cherish his feats against the 'home Unions' more than those in Australia. And that difference in reception, and in Campese's confidence and style, was to be exposed in the sharpest, most destructive way when the British and Irish Lions toured Australia in 1989.

CHAPTER FOUR

OUTCAST

In a way, this moment was virtually predestined. All it needed was a time and a place. Anyone who professes to live life on the highwire, to play their sport on or above that thinnest of dividing lines between triumph and tragedy, has to expect the fall to come.

On playing fields from Coogee to Concord, from Dublin to Dunedin, crowds had seen David Campese throw his 'Hail Mary' pass, that nonchalant tossing of the ball behind him as the defence or sideline closed in, in the hope that somebody would be there to gather it. The title of his own memoirs, *On a Wing and a Prayer*, played up to this very facet of his play. But in July 1989, the reaction to a mistake Campese made on the field arrived with such fury and indignation, such questioning of the essence of the player himself, that he was almost driven from the game. Campese was put on trial: the inquest conducted in public, the verdict delivered instantly, laced with contempt and ridicule in equal measure. He wrote later that this moment 'created a memory of me which I suppose some people will retain to their dying day'.[1] Only recently, coach Bob Dywer called for 'an end to the belittling of Campo' over this particular incident — proof in itself that some remain unwilling to forget, let alone forgive.[2]

But what lent this episode such ferocity was not so much Campese's mistake, but rather the stage on which it unfolded. Campese's error came at a critical moment during the deciding third Test against the British Lions in Sydney. It looked as if the Wallabies might be on the cusp of a famous series win. This was the first time since 1899 that the Lions — a side composed of players from England, Ireland, Scotland, and Wales — had made a tour of Australia, and Australia alone. Since the late nineteenth century, with the occasional exception, it had been the convention for the Lions to tour either of the antipodean rugby giants — South Africa and New Zealand — every four years; although on visits to the Shaky Isles, as in 1971, a warm-up match was sometimes played against Australia or Australian provincial sides along the way. That the Lions had decided to tour Australia exclusively was in itself a mark of respect to the Wallabies' growing prestige over the preceding decade.

This third Test, too, followed a controversial Test at the Ballymore ground in Brisbane, in which the Lions had equalised the series after a thumping victory by Australia in the opening match in Sydney. But in Brisbane the Lions had employed tactics of such overt physical aggression and violence that it became known as the 'Battle of Ballymore'. Australian officials, players, and journalists — with short memories of Wallaby thuggery against visiting English and Welsh sides in the 1970s — cried foul. That tension had raised the stakes for the decider, and the week prior to the Test had seen a feverish level of reporting in the press that carried more than a whiff of the acrimonious debate over the infamous 'Bodyline' cricket episode of 1932–33. The game was also being played at the Sydney Football Stadium in Paddington, in rugby's eastern suburbs heartland. This had followed a two-year period in which Test matches, including those in the inaugural World Cup of 1987, had been shifted from the Sydney Cricket Ground to Concord Oval in the city's west: a small, unpopular suburban ground. Victory over the Lions, it seems, carried the promise of vindication: not only that the game was back in its 'true' home, but to show that the Grand Slam of 1984 and the Bledisloe Cup win of 1986 were no flukes.

Just after half time, as the Australians were clinging to a 12–9 lead, the Lions fly-half Rob Andrew attempted an ambitious field goal. It drifted wide of the posts, sailing into the arms of Campese, who was defending in Australia's in-goal area. At that time of the day — it was a golden winter's afternoon — the sunlight was filtering through the cradle of the stadium's roof, and appeared to spotlight just that part of the ground where Campese now had possession of the ball. Nature itself was conspiring to set the stage. The convention for what rugby players are supposed to do in this situation is clear. Schoolboys are taught from day one: at these times, the ball is to be touched down behind the try-line — grounded — so that play might be restarted from the 22-metre line. That's otherwise known as 'safety first'. It is what players *ought* to do, or what Peter FitzSimons, in his account of this incident, called 'standard procedure'.[3] Only the crazy brave run the ball from behind their own line.

Of course, Campese did exactly that. Since he had been doing it for years, he saw no reason to change now. He was never going to take the safe option. Frustrated at having been starved of the ball for much of the series, Campese now saw his chance. All he could see was wide-open space in front of him, and not only was it there, but he had the ball under his arm, too, at last. A sweeping movement up into Lions territory was on. Here was an opportunity to cut loose and taste freedom again.

But a split second later, Lions winger Ieuan Evans, chasing up Andrews' kick in a way that any good winger should, was upon him. The open space vanished. And with that, the chance to run it was gone.

Campese hesitated, and then threw a pass that simply missed its target — fullback Greg Martin. The ball hit the fingertips of one hand and dropped to the ground, with Martin unable to gather it. The Lion pounced, and French referee René Hourquet awarded the try. Evans, a Welshman, gave his own triumphant, snarling verdict to the two hapless Wallabies, each now looking vacantly at the other. As *Rugby World & Post*'s Nick Cain wrote later, it was 'a great opportunity for Evans, a moment of sheer horror for Campese. Never was the saying *One man's ceiling is another man's floor* more apposite in a sporting context.'[4] It was alleged by journalists that, behind the goal lines, one Australian player, and perhaps others, told Campese in no uncertain terms what they thought of what he'd just done. Neither Campese nor captain Nick Farr-Jones, however, recalls hearing anything of the kind.

But never mind the supposed verballing from his own teammates: much more was to come in the newspapers and on the airwaves. But it came first from the banks of supporters folded in and around that part of that ground. The crowd began baying for Campese's blood, the stadium becoming a hornets' nest of stinging invective, all trained on one man: one man in that corner of the ground. If they had been able to bury him there and then, it would have been done. That it became known as 'Campo's corner' spoke to the long public memory concerning this incident: 'X' marking the spot to perpetuate the public rage at the error.

Campese's mistake gave the Lions a crucial lead at a critical time in proceedings, and, try as they might, the Australians were unable to equalise, losing the game by a point, 19–18. As the final whistle blew, the Australian players dropped their heads, disconsolate and dejected. Spectators filed out of the ground and up into the streets, and towards the bars and pubs. And it was their expletives about Campese that propelled them there.

In the reaction that followed this moment, far more seemed to be at stake, however, than a rugby match, or a Test series. What came forth was a torrent of opinion from journalists and current and former players about Campese's very contribution to Australian rugby, especially his practice of playing in Italy in the off season. But it was much more than this, too. It turned into a referendum on Campese's approach to the game, on his spirit of play, no less, and on the nature of his sporting genius. And what it revealed was a question as to whether Australian crowds had ever really bought into the idiosyncratic nature of this particular player — whether, in fact, they were prepared to accept the inherent risk that came with his exhilarating playing style.

Ironically, it is a fair bet, as his Lions opponents have since admitted, that had Campese kept faith with his instinct, valuable territory could have been made. Jeremy Guscott, the England and Lions centre on that day, recalled that Campese and Martin 'could have started a counter-attack that might have taken them anywhere. We had bugger-all defence at that stage. Ieuan had pushed up and if he had been beaten by the pass then Campo and Martin would have been in the clear; the rest of us were still covering across and there would only have been Gav [Hastings] at the back to try and stop them.'[5] But very few in Australia ever contemplated such a counter-factual result in the period following that Test match. The pile-on began immediately, and Campese was underneath it. And that is precisely where many had been wanting to put him for some time.

The crime having been committed, newspaper headlines handed down a sentence of their own the following day: 'Campo's Agony', 'Campo's Horror in Test', 'Campo's Gift for the Lions', or the simplest of all, 'Blunder'.

ABOVE: Queanbeyan Fourth Grade, 1979. Campese, bootless at far left, maintains it was the year of rugby he enjoyed the most in his career. *Melanie Debenham collection*

BELOW: Against Daramalan in the 1983 Canberra competition Grand Final, 'dashing David' scored all his team's points. It was Campese 29, Daramalan 0. *Melanie Debenham collection*

LEFT: The debutante: Campese in his first Wallaby jersey before departure for the 1982 tour of New Zealand. *David Campese collection*

BELOW: Against Argentina in 1983, Welsh referee Clive Norling said Campese scored the greatest try he had ever seen. *Sydney Morning Herald*

RIGHT: With Mark Ella at training. The two had a near-telepathic link on the field. *Sydney Morning Herald*

BELOW TOP: Goosestep, 'the most outstanding example of individual flair in Australian sport today': even photographers struggled to capture Campese's signature move. *Sydney Morning Herald*

BELOW LOWER: A familiar sight when Campese played against New Zealand: contorted bodies everywhere, having missed their man. *Sydney Morning Herald*

The Sydney Morning Herald

Page 26   Thursday, May 11, 1985

SPORT

SPORTSFILE   Philip Derriman dissects David Campese's celebrated sleight of foot

'Goosestep' a simple but deadly trick

Crowds blamed on team quality

By ALAN CLARKSON

Rugby Union Test winger David Campese demonstrates his celebrated "goosestep", perhaps the most outstanding example of individual flair in Australian sport today.

ABOVE: Campese made the kick-and-chase an art form: it was one of his most devastating on-field weapons. *Sydney Morning Herald*

BELOW: All Blacks v Randwick. A rare sight on the 1988 All Blacks tour of Australia. All Black winger John Kirwan in pursuit. For much of that tour the roles were reversed. *Sydney Morning Herald*

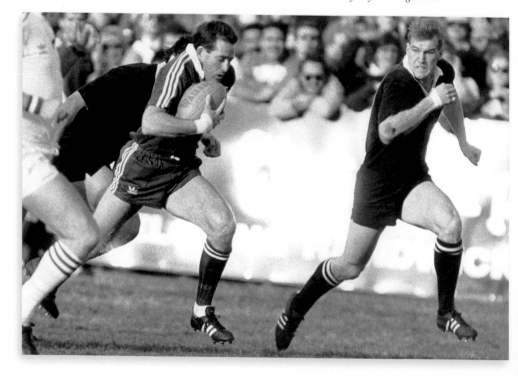

ABOVE: Downfall: the moment when Lions winger Ieuan Evans scored during the third Test. Vilification of Campese's error ensued. *Sydney Morning Herald*

RIGHT: What many wanted to see, but never did: Campese in a Canberra Raiders Rugby League jersey. *Sydney Morning Herald*

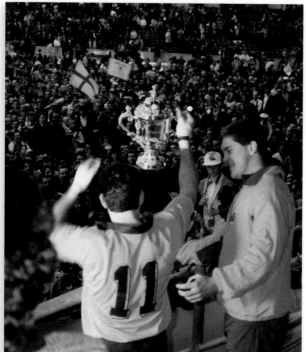

ABOVE: Coach Bob Dwyer said that the first thing that struck him when seeing Campese play was his classical running style. *Sydney Morning Herald*

LEFT: Triumph: Campese holds the Webb Ellis cup aloft following the World Cup final win in November 1991. *David Campese collection*

ABOVE: Advance Australia Fair: singing the national anthem in Paris, 1993. *David Campese collection*

BELOW: Campese could break hearts with his prodigious punt: it ended up costing him his place in the national team. *David Campese collection*

ABOVE: Farewell to all that: Campese salutes the crowd in one of his final games for the NSW Waratahs. *Sydney Morning Herald*

LEFT: Alone: Campese was a self-confessed loner in a sport that prides itself on tribalism. *Sydney Morning Herald*

Rugby writers in the Sydney papers were kinder. Their very descriptions of the episode in themselves spoke to the Campese difference. Having watched him since 1982, they had more understanding of the dangers that walked hand in hand with the dazzle.

Writing in the *Sydney Morning Herald*, Greg Growden observed that Campese 'forgot the coaching manual and did the unthinkable'. But Growden knew that Campese was never someone to be found adhering to any kind of instruction guide or rugby manual — that was against the instinctive nature that had carried him this far in the sport.

In the *Australian*, Greg Campbell's sub-editors inserted a question to frame his match report: was Campese a 'LEGEND or liability?', the capitalisation suggesting that the weight of the judgement was going to land on the former. Campbell labelled the Campese move a 'deadly decision', but, like Growden, he stressed that the Test had really been lost in other areas, not least the inability of the Australian forward pack to match their opponents in muscle and machismo.

In the *Sun-Herald*, Phil Wilkins was less restrained in talking of Campese's 'one maniacal moment ... in an illogical split second',[6] while Campese's 'daring', said Peter Jenkins, simply 'blew up in his face'.[7]

But the venom really came from the Queenslanders in the press and commentary boxes. On the ABC telecast, former Wallaby Chris Handy's thunderous, fulminating call that 'you don't pull on a Wallaby jersey to play that kind of Mickey Mouse rugby' is probably the comment most remembered by those watching at the time. But in the Brisbane press the assessments were even more savage. In the *Sunday Mail*, Wayne Smith went for the jugular, decrying Australian coach Bob Dwyer's decision to 'absolve [Campese's] erratic genius' and asking, 'How much longer can the Wallabies afford to carry a player who appears to feel the mundane, humdrum basics of rugby are beneath his extraordinary talents and who places applause ahead of responsibility to his teammates?'[8]

Writing in the same newspaper, former Wallaby captain and centre Andrew Slack, who only two years before this series had been standing alongside Campese in Wallaby teams on rugby fields in Australia and overseas, was equally unforgiving, and seemed to widen the target, not just from the moment, but to the man himself — to include his character and the kinds of choices he had made about his playing career. Campese, said Slack, had indulged 'in an action that involved a fair degree of lairising' that ultimately 'amounted to group suicide', since the team had been unable to retrieve the match in the wake of his indiscretion. Taking indirect issue with Campese's decision to play the off-seasons in Italy, Slack let fly: Campese, who 'comes and goes as he chooses, makes too many "one-off" bad mistakes when wearing the green and gold. His teammates deserve to be, and undoubtedly will be, disgusted with him.' Slack was not the first ex-player to have moved so quickly from the playing field to the press — nor from camaraderie to condemnation — but his account, admittedly written in the heat of the moment, appeared to be venting a great deal of frustration with Campese that was distinct from the on-field events. Slack was appearing to speak as if he was still captain of the team, as if the authority he had once held gave him, more than most, permission to cast the first stone.

But that Sunday column was only a warm-up to Slack's longer piece that was to appear the following Saturday in the *Weekend Australian*. By this time, Slack had had a week to calm down and cool down. But he hadn't, and he didn't. Under the headline 'Errant genius must be corralled — and controlled', Slack tried to come to terms with the nature of Campese's legacy in the Wallaby jersey. He did concede that on good days there was a 'poetical quality about Campese's talents', comparing him to William Wordsworth, who, as Slack reminded readers, had been described once as simultaneously a 'stupendous genius' and a 'damned fool'. But it was the supposed foolishness that he wanted to apply the blowtorch to. Slack wanted to know 'how often do we see' this 'stupendous genius' in Campese 'when it matters', asking further whether 'it stack[s] up against the number of times he turns damned fool'. He was not, Slack mused, 'looking as flash as the sunnies he wears to training' — a reference to a photograph that appeared in newspapers in the lead-up to the match showing a sunglasses-wearing Campese in conversation with Bob Dwyer.

But when it came to the crunch, Slack was in fact advocating the impossible: what no coach, or player, had ever succeeded in doing where this player was concerned. And that was to pin Campese down, to make him conform — to make him, in essence, just like any other player. Slack wanted to suck the very spirit out of him. If ever there was a moment when the conservatism that had typified the Queensland approach to and administration of the game was bared before the rugby public, this was surely it. As Slack wrote:

> [F]or his own sake and that of the national teams, Campese's errant genius must be corralled ... This free spirit drivel that is brought up is just that — drivel. He is part of a team and if he cannot act that way he is better off playing tennis.

Much was being poured onto the page here. Its essence was the most basic, yet direct, of critiques: Campese had let the team down. But the philosophy poking through that assessment spoke volumes about the emphasis that Queensland sides, especially those in which Slack had played, had traditionally placed on attrition rather than attraction in their style of play, on solidity and structure rather than on style or adventure. It was a pattern of play that, while it had been pivotal to Australian rugby's renaissance in the late 1970s and 1980s, nevertheless tended to emulate more the Northern Hemisphere approach to the game: strong forward packs providing a steady stream of possession to kicking five-eighths, who more often than not opted for safety first — pump the ball into the corners, and wait for the attacking opportunities to come. This was not an approach that placed much premium — if any — on either instinct or impulse.

Another point Slack wanted on the charge sheet was Campese's decision to play in Italy during off-seasons. This move always had tongues wagging back in Australia, over the money that Campese was making in what at the time still professed to be an amateur sport. Never mind that Campese had always had to seek permission from rugby authorities in Australia to undertake these northern expeditions. Slack put Campese's mistake in the Lions series down to the previous 'season in the spaghetti bolognaise competition' that his former teammate had played before landing back in Australia just before the tour officially began, particularly when his mates 'had been slogging [their] insides out' in provincial matches. Borrowing from Chris Handy's on-air lexicon, Slack believed that Campese's 'kicks to the open side to give the opposition ideal counter-attacking opportunities, dropped passes, poor decision making and fragility under the high ball' all 'smacked of a man who has come from a Mickey Mouse competition where he was kingpin and what he did or said, went'.

What was at issue here was not so much the opportunities opening up to some players in this period, but the question of whether, on returning from off-seasons in the Northern Hemisphere, they should have to play a certain number of games back in Australia before being considered for Test selection. As Slack put it, 'If a player wishes to try his hand in Italy, Britain or Timbuktu he should be totally free to do so, but if he intends to vie for a place in the national side he should be made to return for a decent length of time before selection is finalised.' And that is precisely what occurred in

1990, when Campese was not considered for a position in the first Test against the touring French side because of his recent arrival back from Italy. Indeed, as a result of this match against the British Lions and what followed, Australian rugby officials brought in a requirement that players coming back from an international sojourn had to play in at least three games — at club or provincial level, or both — before they could be considered for Wallaby selection.

Campese did have his defenders, however. Bob Dwyer had consoled him in the dressing room, and captain Nick Farr-Jones took exception to the media feeding-frenzy following the third Test. As Farr-Jones recalled, 'It just started to get louder and louder,' so forcing his hand.[9] Farr-Jones was particularly incensed by an article by the *Sydney Morning Herald* sportswriter Brian Curran, who in a column called 'The Last Word' wrote:

> It is possible, too, to forgive, if not forget, Campese's momentary colour blindness on Saturday when he obviously thought he was wearing a red jumper. Perhaps the poor fellow had received a knock on the head ... perhaps he was suffering a delayed hangover from all that wonderful Florentine chianti; or maybe he was just daydreaming about becoming a PR consultant for Taronga Zoo, where his undoubted talents in helping animals, if not his country, will be applauded.[10]

This was enough to move Farr-Jones to write to the *Herald*'s sports editor to express his distress at the 'constant and at times vilifying attacks on one of our greatest sportsmen'. His letter was published in full. Acknowledging that 'Campo's blunder' had been 'careless and costly', he reminded readers of Campese's achievements in the sport, and, significantly, the fact that he had been voted player of the tour by his teammates on the previous year's swing through England, Scotland, and Italy. The players, he said, 'will never forget the whole of Cardiff Arms Park rising to applaud and acknowledge Campese's British achievements during the Barbarians game'. Farr-Jones was particularly keen to point out that two recent on-field mistakes by high-profile Rugby League players, Garry Jack and Michael O'Connor, had not resulted in either the press or supporters dwelling on their mistakes. Why, he asked, 'do we not equally recognise Campo's contributions to Rugby Union and the Australian team?' Then, directly addressing Campese himself, Farr-Jones spoke a very different language from that of his predecessor as team captain:

To Campo I say, 'Yes, one bad mistake on Saturday which I know you will learn from, but mate, if I was a selector you would always be one of the first picked with no handcuffs or chains to inhibit you.'[11]

Farr-Jones knew his players. And he clearly knew the right way to send a message of positive reinforcement to Campese. To have done otherwise, he says now, 'would have been to destroy the essence of what Campese was about. You had to give him a licence to kill, a bit like James Bond.'[12]

The captain had been the only player, too, to have offered Campese words of comfort in the dressing room after the game.

Others also rushed to his defence. On the same day that Curran's article appeared, Mark Ella published his column in the *Daily Telegraph*, focusing, like Farr-Jones, on the philosophy and ethos of the accused: 'a player of Campese's instinct', he stressed, 'is always liable to make errors of judgment. But in the long run, does that make him any less of a player than he really is?' Ella knew of Campese's desire to be the greatest player in the game, and he, too, admitted that the error in that final Test had put a 'dent in that reputation'. Ella felt the need to remind the rugby public that 'to achieve the lofty heights he has always sought he has to encompass some elements of risk'. And he got to the heart of the matter when he pointed out that 'so much is expected from players like Campese that along with every exciting run every mistake is also highlighted'.[13] Later in the week, Michael Lynagh told the *Courier-Mail* that 'dwelling on David Campese's mishap only distracts attention from the fact that the Wallaby defeat originated elsewhere'. Much later, Lynagh put the view to his biographer — ironically, Andrew Slack — that 'the mistake has haunted Campese because he complained for so long about being criticised over it. Campo himself was prepared to say he made a mistake but he wasn't happy about people agreeing!'[14]

Campese did indeed accept the blame. But, as Lynagh hinted, he also kept talking about it. In his own memoir, he devoted an entire chapter to this game, where he clearly wrestled with both what happened on the field and what transpired afterwards in the court of public opinion. The chapter itself shows Campese still jostling with the moment, agonising over it: switching from confession to defiance, from acceptance to justification. He is at pains to give the episode the context he feels it deserved, one he believes was sadly lacking in the ready judgements handed down in the days following the match.

But Campese also sets the scene for his own tragedy. He is playwright and performer in his own drama. Because of the change in playing style from the time of Ella's retirement, he said that even before that Lions series he had come to feel like an 'outcast in senior Australian rugby'. Now it all came pouring out. He did not warm to the 'new revolution' in the game, where winning was all. Wingers had come to be 'regarded as people who can be left out on the sidelines, just given the ball two or three times to see what can happen'. Not only did this make him feel like 'an old relic in the boring games', but a sort of 'old fashioned curiosity, a player to be indulged in once or twice'. But this is hard to square with the fact that across those four years following Ella's departure from the game, Campese had scored twenty-one tries in Tests, breaking the world record in the process. And as the previous chapter showed, his impact on the 1988 tour to the United Kingdom and Europe had been profound. Whatever that tally of tries and applause, though, Campese was clearly frustrated at being left cold on the flanks. The game had become 'far too cautious ... all safety first'. Little wonder, then, that the brutal forward battle that dominated the series against the British Lions left Campese increasingly feeling like he was a bit player.

Accepting full responsibility for the error in that third Test, he marshalled both history and dance in his own defence. He knew what he should have done when that ball fell into his hands from Andrew's boot. The confession here was seemingly total:

> Of course, the outcome would not have been so dire had my pass been respectable, but it was hardly the world's greatest by any stretch of the imagination. The ball caught Martin on the shoulder, I think, and Evans fell on it over the line. There was no way Martin was to blame: it was completely my fault. The orthodox thing to do would have been to belt the ball into touch, of course, but then orthodox methods have never appealed to me very much. Besides, any normal player could have done that. I still believe the idea was perfectly sound; it was just that the execution went wrong.

That in itself was an *apologia pro vita sua*: a refusal to be bound by convention, to be constrained by the rules, by what was expected. It appeared not to matter that this simply wasn't the right moment for chancing the arm. The crowd didn't want Campese on his highwire at that moment: they wanted a team to methodically but mercilessly take revenge on the British pugilism of the week before. They wanted the old enemy put to the sword, crushed. Carthage had to be destroyed.

No sooner had the confession been uttered, however, than the justification — not penance — followed. Ultimately, he could not bring himself to deny his own essence. Full absolution was required, since in hindsight Campese was 'not altogether certain' that it was his fault:

> If you really want to understand what was going through my mind at that stage, you have to look not at that isolated moment but at the entire game. It was another tight match, full of kicking and set-phase play. We didn't seem able or willing to open up the game and my role, as has so often been the case in recent times, was really just one of an onlooker. In such circumstances, I honestly wonder what I am doing out there, standing around getting cold.

Campese would have not been the first winger to feel surplus to requirements. And reading his memoir, with its patient, detailed exposition of what happened, gives the impression that Campese could have summarised it in a single sentence: he just wanted to do what he had always done, what his instinct had driven him to do from his earliest days, and that was to just run it. To have a go. But 'without the ball', he said, 'I'm like Fred Astaire without the shoes. I crave the ball in my hands.' Having failed to have an early settling touch, his 'craving to do something … overtook the logic of safety first'. And wasn't rugby, he argued, supposed to have originated with a 'bloke who picked up the ball and ran'? The feat of William Webb Ellis, he lamented, seemed to have been 'consigned to the Dark Ages'.[15]

Campese's own self-examination over this episode, appearing in his memoir published only two years after the match, was searing enough, and not without its own confected melodrama and hyperbole. He said that he felt like a 'modern day Ned Kelly, guilty of the most appalling crimes known to mankind', and that the 'inquest seemed to drag on for weeks'. He mourned the lack of collegiality in the dressing room, and felt moved to notch a black mark against the country's 'mate syndrome'. Wasn't Australia, he thought, supposed to be a 'place where you stick by your mates in times of strife'? He had not been immune to criticism in the past — it had, after all, been a bollocking from an Under-16 Rugby League coach about his defence in a grand final that had caused him to turn his back on that code for good. And the journalists — many of them teammates or club members at the Queanbeyan Whites — had never hesitated to offer advice in print about where his game could be improved. It was not always dash and daring with 'Mr Magic'.

The Lions series was not the first high-profile match in which Campese had been excoriated for this kind of mistake. Playing in his preferred position of fullback during a Test in Dunedin in 1986, a match that Australia went on to win by a point, Campese had been pinned to the sideline and had thrown a long, speculative pass infield that ended up being picked up by a rampaging All Black centre, Joe Stanley, who fed Mark Brooke-Cowden for a try. 'Oh, that was ambitious,' New Zealand's television commentator Grant Nisbett said of the failed pass. The coach, Alan Jones, is alleged to have told the team in the dressing room after the game that they should take heart, since 'they were playing without a fullback that day'. To this day, Jones denies having made the remark, but Farr-Jones distinctly remembers not only that comment, but also walking into Jones's hotel room as he was giving Campese a dressing-down about the incident.[16]

But all this still begs the question of why the public reaction to this moment in 1989 was so intense and so unforgiving. Seen in hindsight, this was at the precise mid-point of Campese's international rugby career: he had played seven seasons in the Wallaby jersey, but it would have taken a brave soul to predict at this point that he would play seven more. Even so, by this time, rugby crowds, journalists, and especially former players couldn't say that they hadn't been warned that there was a facet of Campese's play that could always unnerve them — that one had to take the rough with the smooth, the sublime moments along with the occasional slip.

The closest equivalent in this period in another sport was probably cricketer Kim Hughes, who, early in his career, was said to have the 'daredevilry' and 'chutzpah' that unsettled both his peers and Test selectors. He was given to the outlandish shot rather than digging in for the longer haul. On a tour of New Zealand in 1977, Hughes had been told by captain Greg Chappell to try 'batting for long periods ... acquaint yourself with conditions'. Indeed, as Christian Ryan observes, Hughes' position at this point 'mirrored Australian cricket's. In one corner sat those who delighted in his fluidity; in the other, those who wished to damn it.' Hughes was said to have a 'wicked grin' that 'creased his young face'. His 'plan was to have no plan'.[17] The comparisons with Campese on many levels are inviting: the carefree, brilliant talent appearing not to know — or, worse, not to really care — when, if ever, the switch needed to be flicked from the cavalier to the conventional. But such an assessment does Campese a disservice: he did not run it from his own line all the time. Indeed, he was already known by this time for his long, raking punt kicks downfield. That, of course, brought criticism from another angle, namely the question of why he wasn't running it.

For Campese in 1989, the sense of occasion — a deciding third Test during a rare visit by the Lions — has already been mentioned. Promotional material for tour matches had featured posters showing a lion head, its teeth dripping blood, footnoted by the catchcry 'It's going to be a jungle out there!' At Ballymore, members of the crowd, on entering the ground, had each been given a small card with the words of the Australian national anthem on one side, and on the other the message, beneath a team photo of the Wallabies, that 'we'll play our guts out if you sing your hearts out'. The message in itself was testament to the genuine surprise occasioned by how loudly the anthem had been sung at the Sydney Football Stadium the week before. All of a sudden, the patriotic swirl around the series had been taken to a level that, until that time, had been rare for the marketing of rugby in Australia.

But it is most likely, too, that the violence on-field in the previous match, and the discussion in the press and among officials that followed, help to account for the feverish reaction to Campese's blunder. As Greg Growden wrote on the morning of the game, the 'build up for this match has been extremely emotional, with allegations and counter-allegations and plans offered to counter violence after the viciousness of the second Test'. There was nothing 'light-hearted ... said about the game this week'. So incensed had the Australian players and team management been about the aggressive physicality of their opponents in Brisbane that an official complaint had been sent to rugby authorities in Britain, with the promise that a 'video nasty'— documented, visual proof of the British thuggery — would follow. Nick Farr-Jones told the press that, so far as he was concerned, it was 'open warfare'.[18]

Much had been made of the fact that three of the Lions forwards who had been at the forefront of the melees in Brisbane — Wade Dooley, Paul Ackford, and Dean Richards — worked for the police in London and Blackpool. This meant, in addition to a tried-and-tested syrup of Anglo-Australian sporting rivalry drenching the daily build-up to the match, memories of empire and colonial subjugation were brought in for good measure. By the Saturday, Bret Harris was beginning his preview of the match by pointing out:

[I]n the convict days the British bullies applied the lash to the wild colonial boys. Two hundred years later, the British bulldog is still whipping us and kicking us around. The British imperialists stuck their boot heels into us when the touring Lions employed organised violence to set up their 19–12 victory at Ballymore last Saturday. Perhaps significantly three members of the aggressive and dominant British pack are of the constabulary. They did to the Wallabies what they do to the Pakistanis and punks back home.[19]

Even allowing for the journalistic licence, this was an extraordinary reversion to the language of radical nationalism, the belief that Britain had long kept its foot on the Australian neck, stifling its independence. Written a year after the Australian Bicentenary, it showed, at the very least, that the standard tropes of the Australia–Britain relationship — not to mention a commentary on Britain's own domestic handling of racial questions after Empire — were very much live currency in terms of appealing to and generating public emotion. Evan Whitton preferred an analogy closer to home, believing the actions of the Lions trio to be 'more appropriate to the licensed thuggery of Bjelke-Petersen's private army in the 1970s'.[20] All of this emphasis on the forward struggle, and Australia's inability to impose itself on its opponents, only reinforced for Greg Campbell 'why we have seen a subdued series from winger David Campese, who has yet to add to his tally of 32 touchdowns'.[21]

With this kind of build-up — Australian players clearly unsettled by what was referred to as 'bovver boy' tactics, complaints being sent to British officialdom, journalists doing their best to whip up a frenzy about the deciding Test, reviving memory and history in a tumultuous hotbed of anticipation and expectation — it is scarcely surprising that when Campese risked all with a hesitant dart from behind his own try-line, or what one British journalist called the 'full Jekyll and Hyde act', the reaction was going to be brutal.[22] On the one side, a visiting team was being lectured by their hosts about playing according to the spirit of the game. On the other, Campese was slammed, not so much for violence — although, in his frustration towards the end of the game, he had lashed out with his boot in a tackle, and struck Lions prop David Sole in the head — but for violating 'standard procedure'.

For all their cherished myths about being the laidback, carefree stirrers of the world, Australians are a rule-abiding lot. Yet one of their own didn't want to know about the rules governing what should be done in any given situation. Welshman Eddie Butler wrote that as a result of the Lions' ability to control the game through the forwards, the 'man who suffered most was David Campese. The seeds of his defensive nightmare were sown in his frustration, even boredom, felt at receiving no passes, at his forwards winning insufficient possession, at the ploys of the men inside him failing to breach the massed ranks of the Lions' defence.' The Lions' halfback, Robert Jones, by taunting the Australian winger with ceaseless high kicks, had 'brought the flying Campese to earth'.[23] Much vaunted at the outset of the series as the player who was going to be the 'Lion tamer', he had ended up being caged by them.[24]

The British Lions players later came to be more generous

in their appraisal of Campese in that series. Such generosity comes easy to the victors, of course, and these were reflections recorded when all the emotions and passions of those seven days had subsided. Captain Finlay Calder recalled that 'we choked him of possession and for somebody like that, who thrives on loose ball and having opportunities to express himself, that must have been torture'. But, Calder went on, 'his mistake wasn't the reason we won the series'. Jeremy Guscott could understand why Campese left the after-match function early, and struggled to understand why he had been blamed for the loss, since 'the man was a bloody genius and tried things'. Forward Mike Teague was similarly effusive: 'If Campese had one of his good days and the sun was shining, you were stuffed. It didn't work out for him on that tour, but he was the best player I've ever seen.' Ieuan Evans simply said Campese was the 'best player I ever played against — a truly wonderful, wonderful player'.[25]

Campese was not for turning. Newspaper reports at the time declared that he had been close to tears in the tunnel after the match. He told some journalists that he was 'thinking about retirement', and there was speculation that already lucrative Rugby League contracts were having zeros added to them with a view to convincing a dejected Campese to leave rugby. In the days following the incident, many suggested that he should not be picked in the final match of the British Lions tour, which was to be against a composite Australian and New Zealand, or Anzac team, a game won by the Lions with the uncanny historical scoreline of 19–15. Campese was picked, but some journalists thought that his 'rehabilitation' might have been assisted had the selectors decided to pick Mark Ella for the match as well. Ella was at the time in the midst of a comeback for his club, Randwick, and while not selected, was surely correct in his judgement that Campese was 'a player who will never change his thoughts on how rugby should be played and I know the majority of rugby fans will hope he never does'. [26]

Just like earlier in his career, Campese was not to be deterred or diverted from his ambition, his true self soon shining through. Even on the Monday after the third Test, he told journalist Peter Jenkins in one breath that while he felt like packing it in, he was a 'gambler, and if I didn't try things I wouldn't have scored 32 Test tries. There's no good going out there and being conservative. If I was like any other player these things wouldn't happen.'[27] This prefigured the judgement made by a British rugby annual publication at the end of the year: 'The wound is deep and may never fully heal, but one hopes that he will have learned by now to treat the rugby journalists on his own patch with the contempt they deserve.'[28]

The punishment for Campese that day came not only from the abuse and vitriol hurled at him by the crowd. It also came from the long arm of the law — but, this time, at the hands of neither a referee nor a British Lion, but of the New South Wales police. On his way home from the match, Campese was clocked driving his sports car at 104 kilometres per hour in a 60 zone. In his memoirs, he recalled driving on 'auto-pilot', wanting to put as much distance between himself and the ground where the lowest moment of his career had just been recorded. Recollecting his emotions at that moment, this passage morphs into recording the kind of sensations he had felt on the ground. It is a dreamy, if dangerous, exodus. Driving his car at top speed becomes a metaphor for what he had been hoping to do when the attempted drop goal from Rob Andrew had landed in his arms. As he cleared the inner city and headed for the suburbs, Campese's mind took over ... and a leaden foot hit the pedal, just as he had been intending to do in the forty-sixth minute of the match:

At that moment, Rob Andrew lined up the dropped goal, but the ball flew away to the right of the posts ... I was past a slow-moving car ... and on to the loose ball. I looked ahead up the road and saw little traffic ... there seemed little defence as far as the halfway line. I put my foot down on the accelerator ... and the surge of momentum in my body as I collected the ball and started to run it out of defence gave me a feeling of exhilaration. And then disaster. I threw the pass, the ball went loose. Evans fell on it and the Lions scored ... and a blue flashing light dragged me back to the reality of driving home.[29]

When he finally did get home, Campese just 'close[d] the door on the world'.

CHAPTER FIVE

MAGIC

There must have been times when David Campese felt that the British Lions were chasing him all over the rugby world, even back to Britain itself.

Two years after the Test match in 1989, as the players from sixteen countries gathered in London for the opening gala dinner of the second Rugby World Cup, Campese opened the official tournament guide to see an advertisement from a British company selling videos of rugby highlights. One of them was a package from that very Lions series, its caption offering punters the chance to 'watch him fumble whenever you want'. It is not hard to see why the joke was entirely lost on Campese, who considered legal action but instead resolved to 'prove what I could really do' on the field. Just as there were moments when things fell apart, there were others, he judged, when 'everything you touch turns to gold'.[1]

That was to prove a prescient coda for a year that would ultimately define him and his Wallaby team.

Campese recalls feeling 'at ease' with himself going into the second World Cup, held in the United Kingdom and France in October–November 1991. Part of this must surely be put down to his having moved on from the tumult and the shouting of his mistake against the Lions. Even some of those who had shouted at him the most over the incident discerned a different player at the beginning of 1991, when the Wallabies, who had ended the previous year by beating New Zealand in the last of a three-Test series on a boggy Athletic Park in Wellington, began the new domestic season by putting visiting Welsh and English touring teams to the sword: the Welsh to the tune of 63–6, and the English — that year's Five Nations and Grand Slam winners — by 40–15. It was this Test against England in Sydney that was viewed by many as symbolic of a side that was reaching its peak. As coach Bob Dwyer recalled, it was the *precision* of the team that day which impressed him the most. He didn't want an Australian rugby style to be all flair with no shape or substance. Rather, he wanted — and he certainly got it that day — 'textbook rugby: sharp, neat, efficient, structured'. Dwyer maintains that his team played better during this game than in any other match that year.[2]

After the England Test, one of Campese's harshest critics from 1989, Andrew Slack, described his performance as the 'best he has produced for Australia in a Test match'. Slack was not resiling for a second from his view that players of Campese's ilk should not be 'beyond criticism' simply by virtue of the flair and excitement they brought to the game. Rather, he wanted to underline the lessons that Campese had learnt. His play against England, Slack wrote, was 'thoughtful, courageous and showed a decision-making process that appeared totally in line with the direction of the team plan'. And by 'courage', he was talking of Campese's defence, not his dash.

Slack now found himself in something of a dilemma over how to assess his former teammate: wanting to acknowledge the change, but not wanting the old Campese to disappear entirely. He did not want to see Campese lose his 'endearing and dangerous' habit of running the ball out from his own line: he just sought better judgement from him as to when that option was on, and when it wasn't. But Slack's new praise was largely because Campese had curbed that very instinct, and by so doing had become a more valuable member of the side, especially since his kicking 'illustrated there is no longer punter of the ball in the Australian team'. Slack's conclusion was that for all Campese's love of the limelight, he also liked being part of a team, and 'Saturday should have proved that they are not mutually exclusive'.[3]

The 1991 World Cup would prove that assessment right. It was in this side that all the planning and preparation to make Australia a serious player on the world stage — a process begun in the mid-1970s, and fulfilled to some extent in the succeeding decade in the United Kingdom and New Zealand — bore fruit. All the necessary ingredients were present: the blend of youth and experience, a core of players who had been there through the 1984 Grand Slam and the Bledisloe Cup win of 1986 — Lynagh, Poidevin, Farr-Jones, and Campese — as well as a number of exciting youngsters such as Tim Horan, Jason Little, Phil Kearns, and John Eales, who would go on to have long careers in the Australian jersey, even winning a second World Cup in 1999. But for all Campese's creation of opportunities for the team, which had never really been at issue — save, perhaps, for very early in his career, when Mark Ella had chastised him as selfish for not passing the ball enough — it was his individual brilliance that was to play a decisive role in helping the Wallabies gain their first World Cup triumph. And there was one match, in particular, where Campese condensed all of his skills into two moments of supreme footballing magic.

One afternoon in Dublin

One of the greatest of all cricket writers, the West Indian CLR James, described the batting of a contemporary, Learie Constantine, in the following terms: 'Every few years, one sees a stroke that remains in the mind, as a single gesture of an actor in a long performance remains in the mind.' The particular stroke he recalled came in 1926, as he watched Constantine play for the All West Indies side in British Guiana against the bowling of Englishman Wally Hammond. Hammond sent down a delivery pitching a foot outside off stump but swinging into the batsman. Constantine's shot in response stamped him 'as a batsman who could do anything that he wanted to do'. He was 'doubling himself almost in two', cutting the ball to the left of point 'for a four which no one in the world … could have stopped'.[4]

David Campese's exploits for the Wallabies against New Zealand during the 1991 World Cup semi-final at Lansdowne Road in Dublin have claims to be seen in a similar light. They, too, lasted for mere seconds. But they also broke through time. These sparkling passages of play, perhaps more than any others from Campese's rugby career, have etched themselves into the sport's collective memory. Replayed before each World Cup, featured in every highlights package of that tournament, and subsequently mimicked in television ads, they have acquired something of a life of their own. On that day in Dublin, Campese was almost insolent in his class.

According to Welsh journalist Clem Thomas, Campese in this game had 'fully exorcised the minds of the Australian public from the nightmare of his dreadful error' against the British Lions. As demonstrated in the previous chapter, the public and press vilification of Campese had been so savage, and so visceral, that he had almost been driven from the sport altogether. But the semi-final in Dublin 'will always be remembered', said Thomas, as 'Campese's match'.[5]

Redemption had come. In the first half of the game, Campese was to feature in two tries that almost immediately took on folkloric proportions: the first, because of the diabolical angle he ran towards the try-line; the second, because of an audacious pass over his right shoulder to centre Tim Horan, who raced around the despairing tackle of All Black wing John Timu to score. Those tries not only crushed New Zealand's team spirit, but they also ended an era of All Black rugby hegemony. As the French rugby newspaper *Midi Olympique* reported the following day, the Wallabies had 'crucified the champions'; the 'sceptre was changing hands'.[6]

The match already had something of a unique feel from the very beginning, as if the normal state of affairs for such a clash had been turned on its head. Both teams were away from home, playing a game of real significance on foreign soil. It therefore seemed almost unnatural, and out of place, when the two fragmented lines of black and gold filed from the tunnel and onto the pitch. The Bledisloe Cup was safely tucked away in a cabinet back at New Zealand rugby headquarters in Wellington. Here were the two antipodean rugby giants facing off in Ireland. They were a world away from the sun-scorched, hard grounds of Sydney and Brisbane, and while the setting resembled more the brooding, sodden grey of New Zealand climes, the teams were meeting each other in the city that poet Louis MacNeice celebrated for its 'seedy elegance', where the 'air was soft on the cheek' and the 'glamour of her squalor' was offset by the 'bravado of her talk'.[7]

And there had been a great deal of talk in the days leading up to the fixture, none more so than the confident dismissal of Campese's importance to the outcome by the gruff, no-nonsense All Blacks' coach, Alex 'Grizz' Wylie. In a media conference before the game, Wylie was asked how his side planned to handle Campese. Well might the reporters have asked, for Campese had been scoring at the rate of a try a match in the tournament to date. He'd scored two against Argentina in Australia's opening game; one against Wales in Cardiff following a penalty-ridden win over Western Samoa; and then, the week before, in a quarter-final against Ireland, two more. For one of them, he had sliced open the opposition defence with such casual yet devastating ease — his sidestep, almost from a standing start, resembled the incision of a surgeon's knife into the midriff of a cadaver. He had, too, that day, despatched a last, desperate pass — more like a fumbled pop of the ball — that had somehow found its way into the arms of his teammate Michael Lynagh for a last-gasp Wallaby try, saving the team from what looked like a certain defeat.

Wylie's response to the press gaggle combined a classic mixture of pre-game overconfidence with curt, but sincere, sportsmanlike decency. He told them that his side's familiarity with Campese had made the Australian winger 'an easier customer to contend with'. It was the twenty-first time the All Blacks had come up against Campese, and again, the reference point for the journalists was the first occasion when Campese had 'dazzled' New Zealanders with his goosestep as a nineteen-year-old in 1982. The very mention of that occasion seemed to be laid in front of the All Black coach as an omen: as if the journalists were whispering, *sotto voce*, 'Remember … this is what Campese can do to you.' It was akin to a warning, even if from well nigh a decade before. But surely Campese had neither the suppleness nor the pace of those days? 'We know what

Campo is about,' Wylie said. 'We know he is dangerous when you give him space. The key is to keep the pressure on him.' The odd high ball booted up into that low, blanketing Irish sky would surely test him, he said.

Wylie was generous enough to add that 'maybe he has done some silly things, but the brilliant things overshadow them by a long way'.[8] In its own way, this underlined the respect that New Zealanders had for Campese, but it was to prove double-edged. Wylie could not have known that his side would give Campese the very room in which he would once more cause on-field havoc.

Even before the match was underway, Campese was giving himself his own space. As the Australian team lined up to stare down the New Zealand haka — with a mere 5-metre space between the teams — he was way behind the fray, cavorting in the depths of Wallaby territory, practising his kicking. It seemed for him a ritual, a purposeful demonstration that he be considered apart — even, at times, from his own teammates. He was tossing the ball to himself, limbering up, showing himself to be at ease amid all the hype of the occasion, and indifferent to the threatening chants of the opponents he had faced so many times. This was not cultural insensitivity, but it might have been a calculated disdain for tradition. As one of the commentators on the telecast thought, 'Campese had heard the Maori challenge so many times that he probably knew the words off by heart.' The former Welsh fly-half Barry John, however, was closer to the mark. Behind all the yelling, Campese was simply 'an explosion waiting to happen'.[9]

Even so, here again the normal run of things seemed not to have the same effect. This New Zealand performance of the traditional war dance seemed to have lost some of its venom and menace in comparison to the blood-curdling efforts under former All Black captain Wayne Shelford. Prop Steve McDowell, the chosen lord of this dance, had the fire and brimstone alright, but there was not the same synchrony behind him in that final leap skyward, not the same bite or spite, not the same sense of a gauntlet being flung down in front of the enemy. Adding to the surrealism, the Irish crowd in Dublin was not disposed to produce the hushed silence traditionally accorded the haka. They fell deathly silent, normally, when goal kickers lined up for a shot at the posts, but not for pre-match war cries. And since in those days no microphone was placed in the heart of that semicircle of ebony to project the sound, this opening act in the drama passed by virtually unnoticed.

In any case, during the week, several media reports had focused on the inaccessibility of the All Blacks to the locals — the New Zealanders had been in lockdown, turned inward, seemingly immune to Irish charms. They were the reigning world champions under pressure. The locals, still broken-hearted from their loss to the Wallabies the week before, nevertheless embraced the Australians. After all, the fabled Irish folksong 'Fields of Athenry' has the Irish waiting, praying for the return of their loved ones sent to prison in Botany Bay. Religion, too, seemed to be on Australia's side. Simon Poidevin, playing in his second-last match for the Wallabies that day, even saw fit to mention that on the night before the match, a mass for the Catholics in the side had been said at the team hotel, and that 'naturally our priest offered the mass for an Australian win'.[10]

Parts of the media, too, seemed to be delivering their own verdict even before the match was underway. Something special was clearly expected. So confident were the tournament organisers of Campese's capacity to pull off the unexpected that they directed the broadcasters to train one camera solely on Campese not just for this game, but for all of Australia's matches in the tournament. So we have the benefit now of being able to scrutinise these moments from nearly every conceivable angle. Photographers, too, have freeze-framed each crucial step leading up to these scores.

Wallaby coach Bob Dwyer recalls that in the first half of that match, the Australian forwards 'smashed the All Blacks into submission'.[11] And no winger could do what Campese did without that momentum. But if a rampaging forward pack cleaving through its counterparts set the scene, the stage still needed its star performer. Dwyer had conducted a team that was orchestral in its collaborative harmony, the moment needing only its soloist to step forward for the virtuoso performance.

Seven minutes into the game, it came. Following a lineout won by John Eales on the All Blacks' 22-metre line, Wallaby five-eighth Michael Lynagh took the ball headlong into the All Blacks' defence. Lynagh himself made inroads of nearly seven metres into opposition territory — itself a testimony to the relentless pressure being applied to this

New Zealand side. But when halfback Nick Farr-Jones heard Campese calling for the ball — the winger had come in blind from the other wing to hover at fly-half — and duly delivered it to him, Campese was still taking possession just inside the 22-metre line. Much work was still to be done. Watching the replay now, one can see Campese in the moments just before Farr-Jones passed, sizing up the defence, looking left, readying for launch. Then, running at an angle that looked almost as if it had been plotted beforehand with the use of a compass — indeed, Dwyer had discussed with him, and demonstrated, the very idea of that angle in training — Campese ran due north-west.[12] Not straight, but north-west, away from the All Black wall in front of him and towards the speckled crowd in Lansdowne Road's Lower West stand.

At first, the viewer at home experienced something of a shock as Campese took the ball. He had mounted his highwire again. Whereas the play had been trending in a certain direction towards the goalposts, the Australian winger took the ball so suddenly — and with so stark a change of direction — that it appeared as if a sudden rush of wind had changed the sway of the play; or as if Campese was some kind of cosmic trail, blazing a new path across a night sky. The watching eye itself was pulled along with him. This was the beauty of the moment: few could have pulled off taking that angle at that speed, and yet the Australians in the crowd and those watching back home were virtually running every step of the way with him.

Campese himself recalls that at this moment, as in all

moments when he ran with the ball, the noise of the crowd faded. He was slicing through his own silence. What faced him was roughly one-third of the All Black team. It was a measure of how much sustained pressure they were under that each of those defenders already looked so haggard, so resigned, almost like passive bystanders to the speed of this lunge for the line. What they seemed unable to grasp was just how rapidly the danger was unfolding. Clearly, each of them either expected this Australian vandal to pass the ball to the support player outside, or assumed that he would eventually run out of room, that the sideline's white chalk would soon put paid to this outrage.

Back in Australia, it appeared as if he was going to run out of the bottom-left-hand corner of the television screen itself. Surely, the reckoning of the sideline would come. He could conjure much, this player — that was known already — but not, it was assumed, the widening of the pitch itself. In those early-morning hours, the leftward shift felt as though it might have tilted the entire landmass, so wrapped up were viewers in following Campese's daring, improbable raid on the enemy's line.

During that mercurial run, Campese was holding the ball in front of him almost as an offering to the rugby gods. But he just kept going, and going, shaping ever so slightly, twice, to pass, but still holding on to the ball. All the while, his frame seemed to angle in towards the corner post, as if some mysterious, invisible thread was reeling him towards it. Something seemed to be pulling him towards the try-line. Soon, with Grant Fox, Sean Fitzpatrick, and Gary Whetton all outpaced — it was as if these warriors had been forced to lay down their arms — only Campese's nemesis, the great All Black winger John Kirwan, remained for him to beat. Three years before, at Concord Oval in Sydney, Kirwan had trampled Campese on his way to the try-line, flicking the Australian away as if he were little more than a troublesome gnat. This time, Campese turned Kirwan inside out: a fatal occurrence for any winger in defence. But by then it was too late.

And he scored, on the outside of Kirwan. To paraphrase French rugby writer Denis Lalanne, Campese had 'planted the try like a cross in the corner of their burial ground'.[13] Andrew Clark, an Australian journalist in the crowd that day, recalls that at this moment, 'the crowd detonated'. Campese, he said, had 'played a double mind game on his opponents'.[14]

Little wonder that by the end of the match, the *Courier-Mail*'s journalist Jim Tucker observed the New Zealanders to be wearing their 'black trimmings as funeral garb'.[15] From the moment Campese took the ball to the placing of it over the line, a total of just under four seconds had elapsed. Had he run in a direct path to the try-line, Campese would have had fifteen metres to cover to get there, not to mention that such a path would have involved running smack into a thicket of New Zealand forwards. Running on the angle in the way that he did — in contradiction of everything he had been taught in the game about running straight — lengthened the distance by at least three to four metres. And yet he got there with blinding speed, seeming to defy the logic of the game of rugby itself. It was a try that, in ordinary circumstances, should never have been scored. No muse has ever gathered the words into a form to do justice to this movement, but Campese moved in the way that Irish poet Seamus Heaney once described the lithe passage of a trout in a stream: it had been 'fired from the shadows' and slipped 'like butter down the throat of the river'.[16] Or, as *Midi Olympique*'s Jacques Verdier reported, 'adventure started on the wing that day', and this try was akin to an 'arc-en-ciel', or rainbow.[17] Momentary, but beautiful to behold.

Watching the footage again today, two points stand out after Campese's touchdown: fellow Wallaby winger Rob Egerton's jump of unbridled joy at witnessing the score, and the nodding head of touch judge Ed Morrison, the Englishman doing so with such vigour that it looked as if he was reassuring himself that what he had witnessed had actually happened. But Campese, as he had always done, simply picked up the ball and threw it to Lynagh for the conversion. For all his determination to prove his separate identity, Campese never indulged in theatrics after a performance. There was never any punching of the air, no heroics, and no celebratory antics. Usually, a smile only. But this time, there was no smile. He simply ran back into position.

In the near half-hour that elapsed following that score, the Australian side had become something akin to the Viking raiders that had once sailed into Dublin Bay with such murderous intent — launching a series of repeated assaults on the All Black line. These attacks took two forms. The first, with the ball in hand, involved wave upon wave of sweeping backline movements from one side of the field to the other. To these sallies, their opponents responded with that relish and unrelenting rigour that has given the All Blacks their history and heritage. Time and again, the attackers were repulsed. The problem was that they kept coming. The second was a series of booming kicks downfield — many of them from Campese's cannon-like right foot — by which means the Wallabies repeatedly turned their opponents around, refusing to let them even sniff the other half of the field. The New Zealanders seemed marooned in their own territory, in a state of near-perpetual siege, unable to escape the Wallaby assaults. At one point, a promising Australian attack that swept downfield again made its way to Campese, and he looked up to see a winger's dream in front: only vacant green fields before him. One more half-step at speed, and he would have been away. But a desperate tap-tackle from the All Black five-eighth Grant Fox brought him down.

The Australians kept pounding away — all guns blazing — but no points ticked over on the scoreboard, since the penalties brought on by the pressure went unconverted as the normally cool Lynagh was struggling to find his rhythm. Campese himself attempted a drop goal from the halfway line, and on the far right of the field, which simply sailed across the face of the goalposts. It was a classic moment of Campese hubris: the dream seller at work. Even the local television commentator for the match, Alistair Hignell, remarked in its wake that 'you feel he can do anything, David Campese, but that was a bit ambitious'.

Campese's wild kick, however, showed that Australia, too, was now feeling the pinch: all that attack, all that concentrated push into the New Zealand defensive line, had resulted in only a small return on the scoreboard. It prompted one of Hignell's colleagues, the former All Black captain David Kirk, to gently — it turns out presciently — chide the Wallaby side, almost as if to spur them on to something special. Kirk was clearly getting the feeling in this first half that his compatriots were struggling to match the intensity of the Australians. He could sense they were not up to the grade, that a once-great team was about to slip from its pedestal. The cup he himself had held four years previously was passing from New Zealand's grasp. It was difficult, he said, to know precisely what to say about the All Black performance: they were meeting the challenge, but gathering no momentum. Speaking of the Wallabies, and no doubt with Campese's bravado in mind, Kirk said there was simply no need for them to succumb to the plague of attempted drop goals. 'I'd like to see them try and create something,' he said, adding for good measure that 'the way they're playing, I think they will'.[18]

What Kirk willed on-air to happen then unfolded before him. It was to come, initially and ironically, from a dropped ball, from a discordant moment when the fine-tuning of this Wallaby team seemed to miss a beat. An Australian lineout just inside the All Black half, won by Rod McCall, was then pulled down and, once more, Farr-Jones looked to liberate those outside him. A long, arcing pass to Lynagh, and from him a shorter distribution to centre Jason Little, looked to once again form the prelude to the building of more phased assaults on the New Zealand defence. But this time a mix-up in the call saw Little throw the ball to no one: he had been looking to his centre partner Horan to come inside. Simon Poidevin, running the lines he always ran in support, was there to retrieve the ball, fix the mistake, and to hunker down in readiness for yet another mauling, the mauling to which he'd subjected his frame over the previous eleven years. The Australian forwards once more closed in around him, a loose testudo to commence its slow advance towards the citadel. And, once more, Farr-Jones was there to pilot some order from the fractured movement.

Then came the magic. This time, too, Lynagh played draughtsman to the drama that unfolded, lobbing a low, pointed kick from just inside the New Zealand half. As the ball floated, then dropped, and bounced once, just outside the All Black 22-metre line, Campese was there to pick it up — and, typically, he did so one-handed. He faced initially the same New Zealand player whom he had left spread-eagled in 1982 when he had scored a thrilling try for the Australian Under-21 side at the Sydney Cricket Ground: Kieran Crowley. Crowley had been summoned from his dairy farm in Taranaki only a week before due to an injury in the All Black squad. He might have, in that moment, wished he was back in his own arcadia, where those he had to manage did not move so fast, or with such unpredictability. Crowley ended up face down in Campese's wake, only this time in the consoling green softness of the auld sod.

As Lynagh recorded in his memoir, it took someone with the 'extra-sensory perception that belongs only to a genius' to have done what Campese did.[19] This time, it was the very ball itself, not the try-line, that seemed to have iron filings encased within, with Campese's left hand seemingly magnetic. Here was one of what Denis Lalanne termed 'the great chemists of the oval ball' at work. And as the play cascaded down that right-hand flank of the field, the crowd gradually came to its feet ... resembling a rolling wave tumbling towards its shore break.

Once again, blackness swarmed around him, only this time Campese drew them in — three players in total — with a right step, then a feint away to the left, then another right-foot step back inside, and then, with the defence confounded but still committed to bringing him down, throwing what must surely rate as the pass of the century, over his right shoulder to a screaming Tim Horan. Campese was creamed in the tackle, but the ball had gone, vanished ... into the waiting arms of his teammate. Watching in real time, it was hard to know exactly what had just happened. Horan had called for it — no doubt — but the verdict was not in doubt. This, too, was Campese's try. No sooner had the pass left his hands than the entire episode morphed into 'that pass' leading to 'that try'. If ever a score seemed to sum up the preceding decade of Wallaby play, it was surely this one. True it was that Australian supporters, in stadiums and club grounds at home, had seen this kind of Campese pass before — times when it had worked, and times when it hadn't.

The New Zealander Kieran Crowley is reported to have told one journalist that when he lifted his head and saw the end of the movement, he had privately sworn to himself: 'You've got to be fucking kidding.' Even in exasperation, there was a grudging respect. Campese, he added, was 'just having one of those days. Everything he tried came off perfectly.' In the words of *Rugby World & Post* magazine, the try had 'defied belief'.[20]

Like so many of the moments in sport that seem to subsequently acquire a life of their own, this one was over in a flash: and yet, as each play unfolded, Campese looked, typically, to have all the time in the world to spare. He was toying with time, making himself its master, seizing the second. Indeed, it was as if Campese took possession of a whole quadrant of the field, declaring himself ruler of its domain, directing all that happened within. His sidesteps were, in the words of one of the French journalists there that day, as if Campese '*s'amusent comme un fou*': as if he was 'amusing himself with his own craziness'. He had gone 'looking for the ball everywhere he was not meant to be'. Here the public had seen a 'beautiful match', in the words of *Midi Olympique*, and borne witness to a masterclass, an elder of the sport handing down his life's work, as if leaving instructions on how he wanted the game to be played.[21]

On that October day in Dublin, David Campese appeared to run within currents of his own making — or currents that had been allotted to him alone — in a force field that his artistry drew from the earth itself. The result was a rugby frenzy of his own creation. The Australian commentator on the BBC call, former Wallaby Bill Calcraft, tried his laconic best to underplay the moment — the pass, he said, 'looked quite fancy, but at the end of the day he knew where Horan was'. This, of course, was true. But it was also no time for the awarding of such modest grades, hardly the occasion for casual understatement. For what Calcraft missed entirely was that even Campese's opponents on the field had been forced into the role of spectators, left strewn by the wayside to marvel. Much like Learie Constantine, no one could have stopped Campese that day: he was simply doing what he wanted to do. To quote Louis MacNeice again, the Australian winger had provided the 'juggler's trick' that 'poised the toppling hour'.[22]

Triumph

For Australian rugby supporters today, remembering the triumph of 1991 has become almost a form of self-torture. The revisiting of the memory brings pleasure and pain: pleasure at the brand of rugby that won a world title, pain at wondering why that style has been impossible to repeat at that level since. The Australian win at the 1999 Rugby World Cup — the first of the professional era — provided a very different set of images: an uncanny drop goal by Stephen Larkham to beat South Africa at Twickenham in the semi-final; Owen Finegan spread-eagling a scrambled French defence at Cardiff in the tournament final. But it would be fair to say that the victors of 1999 do not hold the same cherished place in rugby affections as does the 1991 side; nor that it was achieved with the same style of play. Theirs was a clinical, mechanical march to glory. In part, too, it derives from the expectations that the 1991 victory unleashed about where rugby in Australia was headed. Suddenly, all those clichéd headlines about a coming gold rush seemed to be on the cusp of realisation.

In the immediate aftermath of the win, rugby authorities faced up to the challenge of how they were going to translate the tournament success into commercial opportunities back home. Joe French, the president of the Australian Rugby Union, said that for all the thinking with the heart, it was now time to think with the head — and that meant securing a better deal to showcase the game on commercial television.

Creating a spectacle, it seems, was the order of the day. On their return from London, the Wallaby players were afforded the honour of a ticker-tape parade down George Street in Sydney, something only the Allan Border–led Ashes team of 1989 and the gold-medal-laden Commonwealth Games team of 1990 had received. The doubts of many players before the parade — namely, that anyone would turn up — were quickly cast aside amid a triumphal cavalcade attended by thousands lining the streets, the crowds pressing in on the vehicles transporting the players. The very practice of such parades owed their origins more to ancient Rome than Australian patriotism, but it was the patriotism that dominated.

Campese told the *Sydney Morning Herald* that it was 'quite a unique emotion seeing this today in my own country'. 'Yes,' he added, 'I am patriotic. I'll do anything for

Australia.'[23] Other observers, noting that Campese's vehicle was the only one to receive a police motorcycle escort of its own, and that its progress was at times 'dragged to a halt by the sheer weight of fans draped around their hero', could not resist more exalted analogies — namely, that 'not since Pope Paul VI visited here an odd two decades ago has anyone with Italian ancestry attracted so much attention'.[24]

Elsewhere, there was a certain hesitation that rugby should be seen so brazenly to be celebrating itself. In echoes from 1980, the sport seemed not entirely sure that it should be indulging in all the glitz and glamour. Thus captain Nick Farr-Jones said that his players were just 'down to earth … and a bit shy of the razzamatazz'. They were clearly 'unaccustomed to the heroic role', said journalist Tony Stephens.[25] Joe French characterised the whole thing as 'mild' rather than 'wild', but that was hardly doing the occasion justice, and any sheepishness about all the attention they were receiving seemed to dissipate as the streamers rained down on the players from the buildings above.

Others were not going to be so tentative. There appeared to be unanimous agreement that this team had 'captured the public imagination of the nation'; the *Sydney Morning Herald*'s sports editor John Huxley elevated the victory above the Australian cricketers' Ashes whitewash in England in 1989, or even the America's Cup yachting win in 1983. It had brought 'new converts' to the game.[26] The *Herald* seemed sure — and with good reason, given the flood of junior registrations that followed in 1992 and succeeding years — that 'rugby has earned now the kind of enthusiastic following that ensures it a larger and even livelier future'.[27] Rugby in Australia had never experienced this kind of attention.

And Australians love nothing more than a sporting winner. According to the *Australian*, the game was judged to now boast a different geographic reach: 'from Cairns to Perth and Sydney to Hobart hundreds of thousands of Australians who had never watched a rugby match until the past few weeks forfeited their sleep to watch the Wallabies grind out their historic win' in the final against England. And it was the 'open, attacking play of the Wallaby backline that has really appealed. The skill and flair of David Campese and his colleagues have made rugby fans of millions who before would watch nothing but soccer, Aussie Rules or Rugby League.'

The question was always going to be, however, just how long this euphoria would last, especially given that the tournament had fortuitously coincided with a period in which its rival codes had wrapped up their grand finals, while the Test cricket season had not yet begun. Timing was only one dimension — it was whether the game was going to be able to lock in broader support over a longer period, whether it could truly break out of the Sydney–Brisbane–Canberra axis. Something of this dilemma was captured in an editorial observation about the challenge for administrators, for 'this newfound public awareness of their game must be something of a shock'. The sport now had to learn to live with the millions of new viewers around the country. Even as those words were being typed, a foretaste of the problems to come appeared. This was 'an amateur code caught in a landslide of money'. And how the administrators and players reacted would 'decide the future of the game'.[28]

As these prophecies were flowing freely from the commentariat, the game's authorities were still finding ways to send precisely the opposite message. The Australian Rugby Union refused to pay Campese's return air fare from Italy so that he could attend the parade in Sydney, forcing him to find funding elsewhere. By this time, Campese was well and truly established in a different rugby life from many of his peers — that of the year-round player. He had gone straight from the World Cup final at Twickenham to his Italian club in Milan. This was an arrangement that allowed him to establish the very financial security that the game's officials were loathe to embrace in any open, declaratory way, even if they never refused Campese the permission he required from them to spend his Australian summers playing rugby in Europe.

The whole episode of whether he'd be brought back to Sydney left a sour taste on an otherwise dizzying day for the sport. And so, only moments after the crowd started to filter back to their office blocks, Campese was in a car going to Kingsford Smith Airport, headed back to Italy.

CHAPTER SIX

MAESTRO

In late 1996, David Campese played his 100th Test match for Australia. Before him, only the French centre Phillippe Sella had reached this milestone. That Campese did so in Padova, only twenty kilometres from Montecchio Precalcino, the town in north-western Italy where his father had been born, and where he had himself lived for a time as a young boy, added a deeply personal touch to this prodigious tally. It was, too, a match played at the home ground of the club where he had first played in Italy — the *Campo Plebiscito Sportivo*, or 'people's sports field'. Some Australian journalists, before finding their Italian dictionaries, assumed the ground had been named after him. They came ready to hail this Italo-Australian sporting triumph, arming themselves with tales of 'nostalgia, incantation, escape' for the back pages the following day.[1]

The headlines did not disappoint: 'Campo Magnifico',

'Bravo Campo', 'Campissimo', 'Campo's historic homecoming' adorned their copy, and classical allusions were readily deployed. Writing in the London *Spectator*, Frank Keating enthused that 'Campese of Montechhio comes home alright. The emperor home from his crusades.'[2] And, indeed, there was something of the feel of a Roman triumph to that evening: the player awarded his ceremonial cap with the golden tassel dangling down one side; commemorative plaques struck to mark the occasion; and a lap of honour run at the conclusion of the game to accept the applause from fans.

Prior to the match, Campese had received congratulatory telegrams from the Australian prime minister and the governor-general, as well as from hundreds of supporters, former players, and other well-wishers, many of whom had been moved to write poetry for the moment. As one of them put it, if Campese was a 'rugby god', then this was the 'second coming'.[3]

But there was also a touch of pathos to the observations being made that night in Padova. A chapter in Australian rugby history was ending. There was the sense, wrote one, 'of symbolic closure about the son of an Italian migrant having played his 100th game against Italy'.[4] But with longevity at the top in sport also comes a different kind of status. Campese's name, for so often associated with freshness, dash, and daring, was starting to be bracketed with a certain seniority. The year before, when he had been dropped from the side for the first time following indifferent performances by both himself and the Australian team at the 1995 World Cup in South Africa, journalists had started to call him the 'veteran genius'.[5] It was not quite akin to the words Shelley had penned in his 'Lines written among the Euganean hills' above Padova, that the 'spark beneath his feet [was] dead', but reporting on the game in Italy, the *Daily Telegraph*'s Bruce Wilson concluded that he 'tried too hard and too often to inject some old black magic into the game'. Campese also conceded that he had 'tried too hard in the first half to do a lot of things when I should have just tried to take it easy'. As Wilson concluded, 'some of it did indeed have the mark of genius — the quick hands, especially, and two perfect passes flicked one-handed behind his back. But there is no doubt that, if the eyes still see what other men cannot, the legs do not quite get him there with the old speed.'[6]

Ironically enough, Campese's dropping from the Australian side in 1995 had been on account of his kicking the ball away too much. For one who craved possession, to give it up by booting it downfield was seen as nothing short of sacrilege. As coach Bob Dwyer remarked at the time, Campese 'seems to have lost a lot of confidence in his running game ... Campo must understand that for a guy that we regard as one of the all-time great runners with the ball, to kick the ball this much is excessive'.[7] As one journalist at the time observed, 'the star, it was decided, had finished flickering, and had burned out'.[8]

Even though Campese forced his way back into the national team the following year, one of the selectors who made that decision to drop him, former Wallaby Paul McLean, clearly believed that Campese was past it, and thus should not have been selected for the 1996 end-of-season tour to Italy and the United Kingdom. It would have left the winger stranded on ninety-nine Tests. Speaking to the press before the team was selected, McLean said, 'What benefit is it for us? I believe he's not going to play for us next year so what's the point? It's a terrific opportunity to blood someone else.'[9]

Coming from probably the most famous and decorated rugby family in the country, McLean appeared to have forgotten that the Queensland Rugby Union had arranged a special invitational match for him in 1982 so that he could achieve the honour of playing his own 100th game in that state's revered maroon jersey. Short memories aside, the comments stung Campese, and they still do. Here again was a scion of the rugby establishment, the same establishment from which Campese felt so estranged for much of his career, appearing to thwart the Queanbeyan star marking his century in the Wallaby jersey.

Other officials, however, saw it differently. Dick McGruther, writing to Campese on behalf of the Australian Rugby Union, asked that he be told on the morning of the match that 'whilst rugby has been David's life, he has also given life to Australian rugby'. John Breen, from rugby headquarters in Brisbane, telegrammed more directly that the 'face of Rugby Union in this country would be far different, had it not been for your input'.[10]

Campese's achievement also attracted the attention of editorial writers in the major Australian newspapers: a rarity for the sport. And they came to secure his place in sporting history, to carve his niche in the national and international pantheon. The *Sydney Morning Herald* quoted former Welsh winger Gerald Davies' assessment that Campese 'is the greatest player in the world, ever and bar none'. The *Herald* went on to assert that Campese's goosestep is 'now as much identified with him as the high-flying slam dunk is with Michael Jordan'. His allure for non-Australians was the 'dandified elegance of his play, the outrageous sidesteps and the vision to see gaps and possibilities that other, even very good, players cannot see'. For Australians, his appeal was more straightforward: his 'running genius' had been 'matched by his effectiveness as a match winner'. In a game that is primarily about putting points on the board, Campese put them there with a 'style and a panache that created epiphanies for spectators in all the great rugby stadiums to treasure for the rest of their lives'.[11]

The *Australian*'s editors agreed with Gerald Davies, pointing out that 'these are extraordinary judgments of a most gifted athlete', stressing, too, that 'very few players are ever described in such glowing terms while they are still playing'. Special mention was also made of Campese's propensity to offer instinctive commentary, the 'barb' that helped to make him a 'loner in a game that thrives on gregarious teamship'. That aspect, however, had also given Campese a 'sense of being separate', enhancing his 'mystique'.[12]

'Epiphanies'... 'mystique' ... 'a second coming'. This was heady stuff. But some were prepared to go even further. The Rugby League writer Ray Chesterton, for example, pleaded with his readers to tune into the live telecast of the match, if only to get 'one last glimpse of bliss', especially 'if you always regret you were born too late to see Don Bradman bat, or Bernborough gallop, or Clive Churchill playing Rugby League'. Calling Campese the 'greatest Rugby Union high-flyer since Icarus' — he knew only too well the import of this classical allusion — Chesterton was adamant that 'never again can we imagine such a richly gifted and erratically complex combination of silken skills and outrageous attitude being so neatly deposited by the gods of football on our doorstep'. As the 'Minister for Flamboyance and Unpredictability', Campese was deemed different from the 'aloof Bradman'. For Chesterton, Campese appeared to be more grounded, more real, and more human by sheer virtue of his mistakes: 'We sometimes warm more to people like Campese, who can be fabulous or fragile and treat either circumstance with indifference.'[13]

Campese would be the first to deny his indifference to the mistakes he made on the field, but such writings showed the propensity of journalists to weave new myths as a significant career was coming to a close.

For Campese, the achievement of his 100th game was not simply about marking his time at the top in the sport. Nor even was it about the familial touch that came from his parents making the long trip from Australia to be there for the event, one of only a handful of times they saw him represent his country, and certainly the first time they saw him play overseas. What was also being celebrated here was a professional association that Campese had with rugby in Italy — a connection that had begun some twelve years earlier when, at the end of the 1984 Grand Slam tour, and aged only twenty-two, he arrived in Padova to begin playing for the local club. That made him one of a growing number of players from both hemispheres who were by then living the life of the year-round rugby player. It also made him part of a story in which a sport that had remained determinedly amateur since the early twentieth century plumped for the dollar almost overnight. Campese would remain wedded to his amateur instincts, but he had been saying for years that players needed a better financial deal from the game.

By 1996, too, a new star had emerged on the world rugby circuit, one almost perfectly moulded to fit the demand for a new type of sporting hero in a globalised age. At the 1995 Rugby World Cup, the New Zealand All Black winger Jonah Lomu, while fast and nimble for a player weighing in at 119 kilograms, nevertheless gained stardom neither from running around his opponents nor artfully bamboozling their defences, but from stampeding right over them — sometimes, on top of them. This was a metaphor, surely, for the changes that were exploding onto the rugby scene as Campese's career was beginning to slip from view. The New Zealand rugby press were demanding that David hand his crown to the new Goliath.[14]

Wizardry was giving way to overweening power; ballet, to blitzkrieg.

'Strange new world'

Campese was by no means the first to have blazed a trail on Italian fields. That had begun in the 1970s when a select group of overseas coaches were invited to the country by the Italian rugby federation with one aim in mind: to raise the technical standards of the local game and so launch the national team as a serious contender on the international stage. Thus Welsh coach Ray Bish, Frenchman Pierre Villepreux, and, later, Carwyn James all plied their craft in the Italian domestic league. These teams were mostly located in northern Italy, and usually where the more popular Serie A football teams were not.

A number of overseas players — known as the *oriundi*, denoting an immigrant of native ancestry — were also invited to bolster the competition, the initial wave coming from French and Argentinian players of Italian heritage. In that decade, some Australians, New Zealanders, and South Africans also accepted contracts to play in Italy, and there was 'little attempt', according to historian Tony Collins, to 'disguise the fact that these players were well remunerated'.[15] In Italy, it seems, no attempts were made to hide money in players' boots, as had occasionally become the practice in England and Wales in the same decade.

Two developments in the 1980s brought a steadier stream of international players onto the Italian scene. The first was the shift from bringing in overseas coaches to instead inviting marquee players to populate the Italian clubs, the theory being that their star power in itself would assist in raising the standards — and profile — of the local players and competition. This wave of foreign talent was something akin to that 'band of hotheads' in the opening of Virgil's *Aeneid* Book VI, 'vault[ing] quickly out on to the shore of Italia ... searching for new rivers'.[16]

But this could only come about, as Collins points out, because of the Italian government's decision during that decade to liberalise the nation's tax policies. The ministry of finance 'made it lucrative for businesses to sponsor sports teams and competitions by allowing a percentage of company turnover to be spent on tax-deductible "community projects"'. It allowed fashion brand Benetton to attach its name to 'Benetton Treviso', and, among others, Brecia and later, Milan to benefit from the deep pockets of Italian media magnate and later prime minister Silvio Berlusconi.[17] And it brought in a wide range of foreign players, or *straineri*, including Campese's Randwick teammates Brad Burke and David Knox, as well as New Zealanders John Kirwan, Frano Botica, and Craig Green, along with South African pivot Naas Botha. As one close observer of the Italian game put it, Italy became 'one of the first nations to benefit from the commodification and globalisation of rugby and the migration of rugby talent based on financial as much as playing opportunities'.[18]

Whether the theory of bringing in foreign expertise to help strengthen the Italian game bore fruit remains open to debate. In 1988, the Italian team was thrashed 55–8 by the Wallabies, who were at the end of their tour of the United Kingdom. The local rugby magazine, *Il Mondo del Rugby*, led with the headline 'Australia Fantastica', praising the visitors in their *'maglia oro-arancione'* — 'orange gold jerseys' and *'la continuita di certe sequenze, lunghe e veloci'*, 'the continuity of their phase play, done for long periods and at pace'.[19]

But the celebration of Australian skills — they scored nine tries to nil — could not mask the devastation of the result for Italian players and officials. The nature of the defeat was so shattering to the Italian team captain, Marzio Innocenti, that he resigned in disgust. What he had feared after a relatively promising Italian performance at the first World Cup in New Zealand in 1987 had come to pass. Despite a drubbing by the All Blacks to the tune of 70–6 in the opening game of the tournament, his side had recovered to beat ultimate quarter-finalists Fiji. Back home, however, the Italians simply reverted to type, to our 'old practices', Innocenti said. It was code for a lack of commitment in defence. As Italian coach Loreto Cuchiarelli observed in the wake of the Australian debacle, 'the shortcomings of the national team are a reflection of the limitations of the domestic league', where 'Italian players regard tackling as an optional commodity'. His blunt assessment was backed by Diego Dominguez, the Italo-Argentine fly-half then also playing in Italy, who observed that 'these chaps do not tackle and seem to abhor physical contact'.[20]

Where there was clear consensus among locals and visitors alike, however, was that Italy boasted a cultural experience with its own distinctive touches. At times, that devolved into caricature. Carwyn James equated the Italian approach to the game with existing national characteristics. The Italians, he said, are 'gentle people who burst into emotion much more easily than our players back home. They love the instant comment, the shrug of the shoulders, the volley of words.' This led James to the conclusion that 'their volatile temperament had to be curbed'.[21]

Such assessments, however, did not totally blind visitors to the allure of what was being offered off the pitch. The Welsh writer Alun Richards, for example, recounted his impressions of the Italian game from the time he spent in Rovigo with James in the late 1970s. It was a 'rugby world as intense as any at home', he recalled — high praise coming from a Welshman. This was a different red carpet being laid down altogether, with 'transport, invitations, discounts in leather goods stores, at the tailor's, and prize dishes [coming] our way like autumn leaves blowing down' the streets of their local village. These were the 'gifts of ordinary people, the whole town, and, somehow, always more personal'. It was, Richards concluded, the 'rugby high life'. Match days, too, were something quite different from the 'uneasy air of tension that seems to hang prayerfully in a pall' over the entrances to Cardiff Arms Park. Italian fans were 'better dressed, altogether more exclusive looking', he thought, giving off an air of going to the races. The grounds were decked out almost theatrically, with 'flowers hung in shapely baskets below the entrance … geraniums in a neat pattern set alongside enclosed shrubbery. There was also a Tyrolean band in smart green uniforms, feathers in their hats, instruments of gleaming brass; in all there was a carnival atmosphere.'[22]

It was into this environment Campese found himself pitched at the end of 1984. That he did so was largely due to Roger Gould, the Queensland and Wallaby fullback. Gould had taken up the offer to play for the Petrarca club in Padova at the end of the Wallaby tour to New Zealand in 1982. Initially incredulous about the prospect of playing rugby in Italy, Gould had not found it difficult to acclimatise either to his local surroundings, or to the proximity of the ski fields in Italy and France. However, after having signed a three-year deal, Gould had found himself unavailable to fulfil the final year of his contract due to a pressing work commitment back in Brisbane. To take his place, he recommended Campese to Petrarca's coach, Vittorio Munari.

Gould recalls expressly telling Campese not to mention the money provided in 'brown paper bags' in Italy, the revelation of which would result in him being banned from the sport. Gould even agreed to chaperone Campese to Italy at the conclusion of their British tour. What he recalls from those first days in Padova was a young man with 'stage fright'. Campese, Gould adds, had always been 'very much an Australian ... with all the associated machismo. Yet all of a sudden he is being hugged and kissed on both cheeks by his relatives, men and women'. In the space of days, he was a 'demi-god on the front page of the local newspaper, with crowds coming to watch him train'.[23]

Campese himself remembers that it was this moment that 'adulation' was directed at him. But the clamour did little to assuage the feelings of 'terrible loneliness' and 'trepidation' he was to associate with those first weeks and months in Padova. Indeed, he felt 'like a little boy aged twenty-three in a strange new country', unable to understand much of the language and faced with the prospect of his first, sustained period away from home. The Italian journalist Carlo Gobbi remembers his first meeting with Campese in January 1985, writing that he was *'come un bambino; bisogno dirgli tutto, insegnargli tutto, stargli, vicino se no si perdè'* ... 'like a child: you had to tell him everything, teach him everything, stay close to him so he didn't get lost'. Gobbi described a 'young lad — *uno ragozzino* — with lively, intelligent eyes, which then become mocking and irreverent ... *beffardi e irriverenti'.*[24]

Campese was to find 'sanctuary' and 'shelter' in the home and friendship of his team's coach, Vittorio Munari.[25] Munari, for his part, remembers treating Campese like a 'little brother', but also recalls that the young Australian simply devoted himself to training. He was not there as a tourist, but to totally dedicate himself to his craft. After two games, Munari moved Campese from his preferred position of fullback to fly-half, and while he remembered the Australian almost 'falling on the floor' when he was told of this change, the next day Campese was at the training ground practising his restarts — an essential skill for anyone playing in that position.

Campese credits this experience with developing his understanding of the game and where he might inject himself into the play. It was from this position, readers will recall, that he had scored against the All Blacks in the first half in Dublin. It was hardly surprising, then, that what Munari recalls most of Campese in these years was his sense of anticipation. He could 'see plan A, B, and C like a living computer', Munari said. He 'lived for the game ... because it was in those eighty minutes that he could show others he could do big things'.[26] Soon enough, Munari was telling local newspapers that Campese had integrated perfectly with his Petrarca teammates: '*e uno di noi*' ... he was 'one of us'.[27]

Campese's initial impressions of the standard of the Italian competition conformed to wider concerns about the level of Italian commitment. In one of his first postcards back to his parents, he said the team was 'bloody hopeless', even though they were sitting second on the table. But he added that the 'people are very nice and trying to make the stay very happy'. School was 'ok' — he had been taking language classes — and he was 'learning a bit of Italian'.[28] Campese was not the only one to feel like a lonely Wallaby in Italy. Michael Lynagh confessed to feeling 'very much the outsider' when he first arrived to play for Treviso, asking himself constantly in those first few weeks what he was doing there.[29] Campese discovered other hearths, too, which helped beat the loneliness, finding something of *la dolce vita* that Alun Richards had described. Not a day went by, said Nereo Checchinato, owner of the local restaurant Ai Veneziani, that Campese wasn't there for dinner or lunch. He had practically adopted Campese, this '*ragazzo d'oro*', or 'golden boy', who was polite, spoke softly, always said 'please', and watched his diet carefully, preferring mineral water to wine or beer.[30]

Time in Italy was the great healer. From feeling like being in a 'strange new world', he was later to proclaim that 'this country is in my blood' — his subsequent books even contained Italian pasta recipes from 'Campo's Cucina'.[31]

His time in Italy was readily woven into a tale of the exotic, but it could, as we saw in the previous chapter, also lead to allegations that Campese was bringing back home some of the lackadaisical Italian attitudes to defence in his performances. But there was another dimension to this experience for Campese — namely, the education it gave him in the wider world, a world that he may not have imagined could open up to him when he was a teenager in Queanbeyan. To British journalist Peter Bills, Campese said that the European winters he spent in Padova and later Milan had been an opportunity for him to 'broaden his mind'.[32] To the Italian sports newspapers at the end of his final season there, he said, 'I matured as a man [here]. I learned to know Italy … *ho imparato a conoscere l'Italia*'.[33] 'After a while,' he told another interviewer in 1991, 'the history, the culture, the beauty gets to you. I'm an Australian but it makes me proud that my father is Italian.'[34]

From feeling trepidation and insecurity, Campese was now happy to give his thoughts on the latest performance at La Scala, to wax lyrical about Da Vinci's painting 'The Last Supper', and to give his impressions of the Duomo in Florence. This, too, might have reflected his feeling that Italy, especially after the Lions series of 1989, had become even more of a sanctuary, where, as in the United Kingdom, he did not feel under the kind of pressure he did when playing in Australia. 'Over there,' he said, referring to Italy, 'they're interested in what I think about things. Over there, I fit in.'[35]

This was a powerful statement about belonging. It suggests that Campese's experience in playing his off-seasons regularly in Italy allowed him to not only truly discover but deeply connect to his Italian heritage. This happened in a way that perhaps had not been possible — or not quite so necessary — during his childhood in Queanbeyan. Despite his father's committed cultivation of Italian traditions in a new land, the young Campese, like many others with ethnic origins, considered himself an Australian first. He did not grow up speaking Italian, and despite returning there to live for a few years as a young child, his path to adolescence largely took place within a broader story of Italians assimilating to the host culture, to an 'Australian way of life'. Italy had not really left an imprint on him, save perhaps for his name being continually misspelt or mispronounced.

It is worth noting that Campese was never held up by rugby authorities in Australia as the epitome of the immigrant as hero — in the way that, for example, Robert 'Dipper' DiPierdomenico became for Aussie Rules in the 1980s. Nor did Campese himself seek such a role. It was only later in his career, and then more fully in retirement, that he sought to project, if not celebrate, his Italian heritage.

But there is an intriguing comparison here between Campese and the star Reims, Real Madrid, and France soccer player of the 1950s, Raymond Kopa. Kopa, born in northern France to immigrant parents from Poland, did not try to stay in touch with his Polish roots. As one analysis of his career showed, he 'never tired of stressing that he was a Frenchman'. Like Campese, Kopa was celebrated for a particular kind of game — 'beautiful', 'spectacular', and 'brilliant' being the adjectives most used about him.

His 'dance', 'magic', and 'sorcery' dominated accounts of his playing style; one journalist called him the 'Napoleon' of football, and another praised his 'romantic approach' to the sport. Like Campese, too, Kopa was often blamed for his team's defeats, where limitations in his game, especially in defence, were harped on. But from a family of miners, Kopa also became a symbol of social mobility, an example of how a modernising France in the 1950s — the 'new France'— could allow talent to flourish. Kopa was depicted, just like Campese, as the 'artisan who worked at his game', thus illustrating the 'hard path by which those born at the bottom might ascend the social ladder'.[36]

Campese's blend of natural talent and his capacity for hard work was noticed from the very start of his career. Like football for Kopa, rugby was a way out — in the case of Campese — of working-class Queanbeyan: a means, as he had put it earlier, to 'do something with my life'. His Italian sojourns were to set him up financially for his immediate post-playing life, but they were also clearly a means of discovering his own identity.

'Rugby's my life'

The offer to play rugby in Italy came just at the right time for Campese. In the eyes of many observers of the game, from the moment he started to make an impact on the club scene in Canberra, it had been a question of when, not if, he would make the jump to Rugby League, thereby following in the footsteps of Wally Lewis, Ray Price, and Michael

O'Connor, among others. So it was that, at the beginning of 1984, Campese made known publicly his interest in switching codes. Speaking to the *Daily Mirror,* he stressed that he just couldn't 'afford to go along the way I am … I'm just not earning enough money to do what I want to do, and I simply cannot afford not to consider turning to League.' He made it clear that he would accept the best offer available, and that Seiffert Oval, headquarters of the Canberra Raiders, would not necessarily be his new home. Counting out the number of rugby Tests he would likely play that year — with three against New Zealand, alongside tours to Fiji and the United Kingdom, Campese calculated that he would be without pay for eighteen weeks or more. And by then, with twenty Tests under his belt, he'd be 'looking for a change'.[37]

This was less an attraction to Rugby League being aired than it was a reflection of the financial realities he was facing. For players such as Campese, the calculation was simple: the more representative games he played, the more detrimental it was to his job prospects. Having left school at sixteen, and with no university qualifications, Campese found himself in a different position from many of his teammates in the Australian Capital Territory and, later, New South Wales and Australian sides. While they were simultaneously working in their chosen professions and chasing promotion and advancement in the fields of law, medicine, or education, Campese was taking a string of jobs, primarily designed not to establish his future, but to allow him time to train.

It was perhaps for this reason that Campese, speaking after his retirement from the game, classified himself as a 'rugby professional', not a 'professional rugby player'.[38] British rugby historian Sean Smith mused:

[D]epending on your point of view, [Campese] was probably the last entertainer of the amateur game or the first of the professional. He combined many of the best qualities of both. He respected the traditions of a beautiful game but brought to it levels of fitness, skill and dedication that were scarcely possible in the old days of Saturday afternoon rugby.[39]

Bob Dwyer is one of a legion of former coaches and players to speak in near-reverential tones of Campese's 'phenomenal self-discipline' in his approach to diet, as well as in his speed, skill, and strength training.[40] But it was these very demands on players at Campese's level that fed growing calls for the game's officials to think seriously about some form of financial compensation for them.

What it meant, too, was that, when certain opportunities presented themselves to players of his calibre, particularly those related to playing in South Africa, the moral calculus in making certain decisions could be pushed to one side with seeming ease. In 1985, Campese, along with Wallabies Roger Gould and Glen Ella, decided to accept an invitation to play in an international seven-a-side tournament in Durban. Ella's going, as an Indigenous Australian, dominated the headlines. His last-minute decision to do so involved a scramble to Mascot from his house in Matraville, clutching only football boots and a bag: itself testament to the agony of deciding whether or not to go, given the intense family and public pressure. Ella's brother Gary, then working for the Department of Aboriginal Affairs in Canberra, had publicly rebuked his brother for even contemplating the trip, and the wrath of other Indigenous commentators and leaders duly followed.

The move was roundly criticised by the Australian press, and appeared to contravene the 1977 Gleneagles Agreement, whereby Commonwealth countries had agreed not to play sport in South Africa as a means of maintaining pressure on its apartheid system of government. That the visit took place, too, after yet more shocking scenes of the South African government's brutal suppression of protests against the system only fuelled the public debate over this incident. Despite pleas from the Australian Rugby Union president, Nick Shehadie, to the players not to go, the union ultimately absented itself from any responsibility for the players' involvement by underlining that they were going not as national representatives but as individuals; at the airport before their departure, Roger Gould told the press that the trip was 'personal business'.

The *Australian* newspaper did not see it the same way, editorialising that the trio were 'wrong to go to South Africa … this is just not the time to imply any approval for events in that country'. Acting foreign minister Gareth Evans stated that a visit to South Africa would be claimed by its government as a breakthrough from its sporting isolation. It was a 'matter for regret', he added, that the 'three players, wittingly or not, should be giving the South African government such aid and comfort. It comes at a time when the rest of the civilised world is expressing its revulsion at the Botha government's apartheid regime and its failure to move towards genuine reform.'[41]

Sure enough, the reaction in South Africa was as Evans had predicted: one of the country's most prominent rugby writers described a 'feeling of elation' at the arrival of the three Australian players. 'From our point of view,' added Ted Partridge, 'this is the big, big breakthrough that everyone has been waiting for.' From the other side of the divide came denunciation, with the president of the South African anti-apartheid Council of Sport declaring it to be 'most inhuman to come and play rugby here while the whole of South Africa is being tear-gassed and shot by apartheid gone mad'.[42]

Campese maintains that he went for the rugby alone, that his going was not a political statement about the South African system. But this was the easy way out — although one defended by the opposition leader at the time, John Howard, who said it was not his job to 'comment on the actions of indviduals' who were not going as representatives of their country, and by Queensland premier Sir Joh Bjelke-Petersen, who retorted that 'surely governments are not the only ones with a conscience'.[43] Clearly, however, the controversy surrounding the decision appears to have had an effect on Campese. On his arrival back in Australia, he refused to comment to the press about the visit, and asked a spokesman to simply say that he had 'a heavy cold and is tired'. The *Canberra Times* reported the statement underneath a headline that appeared only once in his career: 'Campese quiet'.[44]

As his career progressed, however, Campese's star power in the game and his preparedness to offer raw and unscripted copy to journalists led him to become more audible than many others on the question of financial recompense. This put him in a unique position. Unlike most other players of his era — save for Farr-Jones and Michael Lynagh and, later, centres Tim Horan and Jason Little — Campese was an Australian rugby player of whom it could be said that he was not just a player, but a brand. And while it is true that his brand power was not the equivalent of an Allan Border, Steve Waugh, or Mal Meninga, his on-field exploits and off-field expressiveness cultivated a wider appeal than any other Australian rugby player of any generation, before or since. When interviewed for this book, Roger Gould specifically pointed out that Campese's very lack of 'nuance and social expectation', although it ruffled officialdom, put rugby squarely on the back pages of the newspapers, making it at least competitive in the most-saturated winter football market in the world.

By the early 1990s, the Wallabies' World Cup success and Campese's starring role in that tournament had pushed him even more to the forefront of media attention. If rugby was affectionately known as the 'game they play in heaven', he became the 'name they say in heaven'. More and more, he was depicted as a rugby troubadour, the star driving a BMW with number 11 plates and the beneficiary of sponsorship deals with Adidas, who provided his boots, and with Pepsi, Sony, and Speedo — who, for publicity purposes, filmed him running with a ball underwater.

He had released a memoir, *On a Wing and a Prayer*, in 1991, ghostwritten by English journalist Peter Bills. By 1994, Campese had opened his own sports stores on the north shore of Sydney, designed his own fashion brand — named after the 'goosestep' — and was even being courted by the worldwide sports-management firm MGM to do a Pele-style world tour in which he would play exhibition matches and offer coaching clinics. The latter idea never got off the ground, but it gives an indication of the level of interest that Campese was generating in the sport. As Philip Derriman noted in early 1993, 'Campese is in the curious position of having become a rugby legend before ceasing to be a rugby player, rather as if he had been canonised before dying.'[45]

So, along with playing in Italy — Campese in his first season with Petrarca made $15,000, and $20,000 in the second, rising to $135,000 per season when he joined Berlusconi's Milan — and the kinds of endorsements and sponsorship deals he was attracting, Campese could certainly air his grievances about money matters in rugby from a position of financial security. At the very least, it was not at all surprising to hear him argue the case in 1994 for players to be allowed to trade on their names.[46]

But that didn't stop League scouts from waving sizeable cheques in front of him, the most high-profile being the

English League club St Helens, which in 1988 offered Campese a then staggering sum of close to $275,000 a season. He was later to disclose, too, that in addition to Canberra, three other clubs — Manly, Canterbury, and the Gold Coast — all came knocking at various stages throughout his career. He hid nothing in telling readers that when such approaches came through, and in particular that from St Helens, he thought much about 'memories of home, of my childhood, of our regular shortage of dollars'. He was conscious, too, of the implicit sneer from those who assumed that the 'circumstances of [his] upbringing' would influence every decision he made about these questions.[47] But even in 1991, he wrote of the memories of League's booze culture, and of the wound inflicted by his coach back in the late 1970s, when the local side lost its grand final and he was made the scapegoat for defensive lapses. It was a world to which he did not wish to return.

So the subject of Campese and professionalism is complicated. It is possible to see him as one of a number of higher-profile players around the world who encouraged the game's hasty, if hesitant, embrace of professionalism, yet who, while doing so, maintained consistently that rugby was at risk of losing its special camaraderie and spirit. For a player so long associated with the breaking of conventions and rules, he was to become — and remains still — a champion of the amateur ethic. Campese never advocated pay for play, but he believed that players should be entitled to some share of gate takings at the end of their careers in the form of a trust fund — 'a sort of golden handshake' — and that the

Australian Rugby Union was simply not 'putting Union into the marketplace' to compete with the 'blanket coverage' that Rugby League enjoyed. When Campese described the Winfield Cup being as 'synonymous with Australia as hats with corks and tins of beer', it gives an insight into the envy that players of his ilk felt as they looked over the fence at the mass following that League had attracted.[48]

For Campese, however, the issue of substance was the generational gap in how the game was being managed as its feet were stepping ever so gingerly onto commercial terrain. There was 'too great a gulf in views and attitudes', he wrote, 'between those who administer the game and those who actually play it'.[49]

Campese's sentiments were illustrated dramatically in the Northern Hemisphere when, in March 1991, following their Five Nations match against Wales in Cardiff, English players decided to boycott the after-match press conference. The move had come in protest, so the players said, over the incessant demands of the London press for access to them. That reason was widely dismissed as a smokescreen for continuing frustration among the team at the lack of funds trickling down from head office and into their pockets.

What made this particular incident all the more noteworthy was that the International Rugby Board had just agreed to some relaxations to the regulations around amateurism. The problem, however, was that few could interpret them with any confidence. Thus the Rugby Football Union's secretary, Dudley Wood, was the first to admit their lack of clarity. Accordingly, Barclays Bank could pay a player £300 to speak at a dinner, or a supermarket could ask a player to cut the ribbon at its opening, but a player was not permitted to appear in uniform and comment on the game, or gain any financial reward for appearing at a rugby-related occasion. Likewise, Michael Lynagh could appear in television ads spruiking shampoo, but Campese could not display a picture of himself in a Wallaby jersey in the front window of his sports stores. Even so, *Rugby World & Post's* Mick Cleary could still conclude, in the wake of the English player revolt, 'It's too easy to state categorically that the players want a share of the money, although that sort of feeling is in the air somewhere. The players do not seem quite sure as to exactly what they want. All they know is that there is money in the game and that they are not seeing any of it.'[50]

The extraordinary success of the second World Cup in Britain at the end of 1991 only raised the stakes even further. Whereas the first tournament held in Australia and New Zealand four years before had generated a profit of approximately $3 million — barely enough to cover the costs of staging it — the event jointly hosted by the United Kingdom and France in 1991 doubled that amount, while the profit from the 1995 event soared to just under $60 million.

As the second captain to hold aloft the Webb Ellis trophy, Nick Farr-Jones was often asked just how long money could be kept at bay from the game. In 1992, his team had just signed with the International Marketing Group (IMG), a sports-marketing firm, to manage its own publicity and other commercial enterprises. But Farr-Jones was also proposing that players be put on a retainer by the Australian Rugby Union. While unsure of the precise figures — those he came up with were small beer indeed ($8,000, $12,000, or $16,000 per player per season), barely what Campese had received for five months' work in Italy in 1984 — his primary complaint echoed that of his teammate eight years before: 'I'm only in the office for nine months in the year. What about the other three months?'

Like Campese, Farr-Jones was not suggesting pay for play — even though, following a lengthy interview on the subject, journalist Jim Tucker opined that his suggestions toppled easily into that territory. Much like others who had suggested similar schemes, Farr-Jones's ideas ran into an official brick wall. Norbert Byrne at Australian rugby headquarters dismissed the proposal as 'fairyland'.[51] This, at a moment when rugby's profile in the country had never been higher. Farr-Jones maintained, however, that the last he had heard, 'the Eiffel Tower hadn't collapsed and neither had Rome been sacked by pagans because of money perhaps changing hands in return for playing rugby'.

That rugby's amateur ethos crumbled quickly is not at issue: by 1995, a number of forces combined to force the hand of officialdom, not least of which was the return of South Africa to international rugby, along with a civil war that had started in the thirteen-man code early that same year, when Rupert Murdoch's News Limited's proposed 'Super League' was rejected by the Australian Rugby League. That started a bidding war between rival camps. It meant that Rugby Union players were now even more of a target for League scouts than they had been in the 1980s and early 1990s, when players of the calibre of Ricky Stuart, Brett Papworth, Andrew Leeds, James Grant, Scott Gourley, and later Garrick Morgan made the jump. As New Zealand Rugby Union's Richie Guy stated, 'We don't want our players sitting there like lambs to the slaughter. The advent of Super League could force us to move to professionalism much quicker than we were going.'

In Australia, the turmoil in Rugby League prompted rugby officials to approach News for a deal, and just two days before the playing of the Rugby World Cup final in Johannesburg, the South African, New Zealand, and Australian unions agreed to a ten-year, US$550 million deal with News — a figure that inaugurated the Super Rugby and Tri Nations competitions.[52]

That announcement, however, followed what *Sydney Morning Herald* sportswriter Peter FitzSimons termed the 'rugby war', in which a Kerry Packer–backed 'World Rugby Competition' (WRC) appeared to be on the brink of securing the future of the game. While Campese was not one of the players originally approached by the WRC — he was, after all, widely believed to be coming to the end of his career — he liked what he heard when briefed about their vision for the game. Players would be paid reasonably, and rugby would be 'run as a professional business, not like some private boys club'. He eventually signed with them — one of the last players to do so. Although it failed, Campese was sure that it 'basically forced the establishment to go professional. The days of amateurism and shamateurism were finally over.'[53]

What remains at issue is rugby's management of this seismic change. As Michael Aylwin and Mark Evans argue, 'By holding off until basically the 21st Century, by which time the information age had properly taken hold, professional rugby was forced to establish itself in a more demanding, consumer-led culture than other sports had contended with during their conversions.' Sheer quantity across all aspects of the game — dollars, matches, and sponsors — overtook quality in a 'headlong rush'.[54]

Lacrimae rerum ... or the 'tears of things'

Campese already sensed a new age coming with the advent of professionalism. His response came in two forms: one, a readiness to prepare himself for a different kind of physical challenge; the other, to appeal to the very sentiment he felt was slipping from the game's grasp: loyalty.

Prior to the 1995 World Cup, journalists were noting with intense interest Campese's increase in physical size. The will-o-the-wisp was well and truly leaving behind the lithe form that had slipped onto Christchurch's Lancaster Park in August 1982. He had weighed in at 79 kilograms on that occasion, and over the years his weight remained steady; even at the 1991 World Cup, he was still only 82 kilograms. But by 1995 he had bulked up to 91 kilograms, an increase that brought the attention of drug-testing authorities. *Inside Sport*'s Mark Abernethy, profiling Campese before that tournament, said that he looked 'more like a solid oak door', his bulk now putting him in the 'John Kirwan league of wingers who can smash straight through their man if the need arises'. Abernethy was not the only observer to greet the change with incredulity. Could anyone, he wondered aloud, 'ever really envisage Campese being known for sheer brute force'?[55] Asked what drove him to pump the extra iron at this stage of his career, Campese's response was straightforward: 'I hate the fear of failing.'[56] It might also have been the fear that if he failed to add the bulk, the sport that was his life would leave him behind.

But Campese's weight gain was also a recognition of realities — the game was changing. Players were simply becoming bigger, defences more organised, breakouts harder to initiate. He seemed always to have had to line up against All Black wingers, in particular, who dwarfed him in terms of sheer bulk — first a rampaging John Kirwan, then a bullocking Va'aiga Tuigamala, and then the giant Jonah Lomu. And that was before the lawmakers had their say. New rules introduced in 1992 were judged by many — with all the hyperbole that so often comes with change — as heralding the 'death of the game'. In short, they meant 'there was now little purchase in trying to run the ball for the simple reason that the penalty if you fail to sustain the movement is too great'. Or, as former All Black coach Grizz Wyllie put it:

We all want to encourage the winger to have a go for the corner. It's the classic movement of the game. Not anymore. So the winger has a go, gets tackled, the ball is trapped, and the attacking side loses possession. The defence then kicks 50 yards downfield.

The changes were widely regarded by coaches and players, and even by some referees, as a blow to continuity, and clearly made some teams and players opt more for the older territorial tactics — for that, read kicking — than adventurous play.[57] Campese recalls that he became 'more conservative' in his last couple of seasons, a point of agreement with his coach, Bob Dwyer. 'When you get a bit slower,' he added, 'you tend not to take so many risks, knowing that you don't have the speed to get yourself out of any tricky situations. I had been in that limit-your-mistakes mindset ... compromising my own ideals.'[58] Gone, it seems, was the 'young kid who went out there and just wanted to run from anywhere. In those days my attitude was, "OK fellas, just follow me. I don't know where I am going, but follow me."'[59]

This, however, understates the changes in Campese's own game. Much as fast bowlers often become more adept at swinging the ball towards the end of their cricket careers, Campese developed an ability to inject himself into the game at critical moments, providing the crucial pass, creating spaces for others. His speed might have gone, but he could still read the play better than most around him.

Still, it was the creeping conservatism in Campese's play that saw him dumped from the side before a Bledisloe Cup Test against the All Blacks in July 1995. No fewer than three morning newspapers in Sydney marked the sacking with headline posters to adorn the footpaths outside newsagents. Again, no other Rugby Union player had been accorded that kind of media treatment. Campese's response, after trotting out the standard lines about sport being unforgiving, was to stress his loyalty to the game. Indeed, it was the Rugby League bounty he had refused that he thought gave him almost a mortgage on his wing spot. 'I have been very loyal to the Australian Rugby Union for the past thirteen years,' he remarked. 'I didn't go to League — I didn't want to go to League — because I enjoy rugby. And I try and help them out as much as I can when they want something done.'

His gripe was not so much about the wielding of the selectors' axe, as it was about the telling of it: Campese had heard the news not from Dwyer, but from a press photographer at the airport. 'It's not very nice,' he told journalist Liz Van Den Nieuwenhof. 'And then you start to think about how loyal they are to me.' He then pointed to the scoreboard. 'No matter how many tries you score ... it means nothing.'[60]

The *Daily Telegraph-Mirror* held a snap poll of fans, who, they reported, overwhelmingly favoured 'Campo', with supporters of all ages voicing their claims for his retention in the side. Still, he was in a place where ultimately no top sportsperson wishes to be: the object of sympathy, even pity. Alan Jones thundered that the decision was an 'affront' and, curiously, marshalled as supporting evidence not Campese's exploits on the 1984 Grand Slam tour, or even at the 1991 Rugby World Cup, but rather his try for the Australian Under-21s at the Sydney Cricket Ground back in 1982: as if freeze-framing the star at the moment he burst onto the international stage conferred its own rights to permanence in the team. These encomiums aside, Campese had, nevertheless, become the 'sacked hero', rugby's 'greatest entertainer' dumped in just 'three minutes'.[61]

That match in 1982 was also on Spiro Zavos's mind. He, too, was returning to the creation myth. Watching Campese earlier that season in 1996, playing in Sydney for New South Wales, Zavos could not but help observe the coming twilight: Campese was unable to find touch with his kicks, and 'when he tried to run, he was cut down before he could spreadeagle the opposition'. Zavos had been an unabashed devotee of Campese since seeing him play in that match for the Under-21s. He had written columns hailing him as the successor to the Union, then League great, Dally Messenger. But, 'unlike Messenger', Zavos added, Campese 'stayed true to the faith'.[62]

On that March night in Sydney, one of the final times he saw Campese play, Zavos, too, reached for the classics to make sense of the moment. 'The instinct to do the fabulous was still there — as it will be for as long as he plays. But the genius that worked off that instinct is fading,' Zavos remarked. Walking out of the Sydney Football Stadium that evening, he thought equally of the tragic death at a young age of his friend the journalist Wanda Jamrozik, and also of Campese's last hurrah. 'A Latin phrase came to my mind, *lacrimae rerum* — the tears of things — Virgil's gentle warning about the fragility of life and wondrous talent.'[63]

Campese would have to deal once more with the hurt of being dropped from the Australian team on that final tour to Britain in 1996, when, after the euphoria of Padova, coach Greg Smith omitted him from the match against Scotland at Murrayfield, one of the remaining two Tests on the trip. That left Cardiff Arms Park — perhaps fittingly — as the location of Campese's final Test; Twickenham was to be his last appearance in the Wallaby jersey. But it was always, too, the moment he feared. In Cardiff, he told journalists that 'my life's been with the Wallabies. To see the guys go round next year, to watch them play, it's going to hurt.' In the match program, British rugby journalist John Kennedy affirmed that 'no-one, but no-one, from outside of Wales' had a 'greater affinity with Welsh rugby supporters'.[64]

After a final lap of applause the following week at Twickenham, where he scored a try that saw the crowd 'explode', he said simply that 'it was pretty sad'. Once more, his contribution was classified as 'old magic', regathering a chip kick and then 'sending a teammate away with a cunning reverse pass'.[65] But the real farewell had been in Cardiff. Promotional material for the match farewelled him as an Italian and an Australian by saying 'Arrivederci Campese'. As the final whistle blew, and after the congratulatory handshakes from referees, opponents, and his own team, Campese 'stood alone', noted one report, 'and gave a modest wave and a brief round of applause to the true rugby people, on their feet and cheering this one-off man. He was as gracious and stylish as you would hope.' Before the end of the match, he had delivered a 'calming but stern lecture' to a team that was starting to lose faith in itself. As Bruce Wilson recorded, this was 'his last great service to Australian rugby, and a fitting one. Viva!'[66]

CONCLUSION

AMID THE RUBBLE

In July 2020, a curtain came down on a small but significant part of Australian rugby history. Sydney's Concord Oval, the former home of the Western Suburbs rugby club, the New South Wales Waratahs, and the Wallabies, and a ground that had co-hosted the first Rugby World Cup final in 1987, was demolished. Once planned to be the Australian equivalent of some of the renowned rugby stadiums around the world, it was now being turned into a community recreation facility. But there were no television cameras at Concord to record its demise, no reports in the newspapers, no comments from either Rugby Australia or the New South Wales Rugby Union on the pulling-down of the stadium.

And perhaps for good reason. The ground had long failed to generate affection among the rugby public. The list of grievances was long: the first, its location. Never mind its position in an area then starting to be pinpointed on city maps as the demographic heart of Sydney. The grievance was cultural, visceral. Situated on Parramatta Road, it was a world away from the more salubrious climes to which rugby afficionados were accustomed, those of Moore Park — where the Sydney Cricket Ground (SCG) sits adjacent to the swank pubs and restaurants of nearby Paddington. As Greg Growden asked in 1986, would the rugby devotees from Sydney's east and north 'have the gumption to get in their Volvos and BMWs and head in a seemingly foreign direction? Would they take their hub caps off when they got there?'[1]

The second was capacity. The ground held just 25,000 spectators: fine for a provincial match, laughable for an international, let alone a Rugby World Cup or Bledisloe Cup match. Spectators in the eastern grandstand looked straight into the sun; those on the western side had to angle their necks around bizarre, twig-thin steel cables that wobbled from rooftop to seat row, bisecting their view of the pitch. At Test matches against New Zealand, more All Black than Wallaby supporters crammed onto the grassy hillocks at either end of the ground. In effect, their sheer numbers, not to mention their exuberance, negated any home advantage for Australian teams. No Wallaby side had ever beaten New Zealand there.

The whole exercise, too, had the somewhat foul odour of white-collar crime hanging over it. Ken Elphick, the official in charge of the project, was found guilty of defrauding the New South Wales Rugby Union, and served two-and-a-half years in prison for doing so. It is hardly surprising, then, that no one from rugby officialdom came to witness the ground's reduction to rubble.

Like many of his contemporaries, Campese had been no fan of Concord: he described it once as 'unloved' and 'unlovely'. How anyone, he asked, 'conceived that place as the future home of international rugby is beyond belief; always was beyond belief of the player'. His judgement was typically forthright: the 'whole thing was a disaster from start to finish and a shocking indictment of the stubbornness and intransigence of people in authority'. As a final flourish, he added that the ground was always going to be a 'graveyard'.[2]

Yet, viewed from today's perspective, the very idea of Concord Oval doesn't seem as far-fetched as it might have back then. Rugby had until that time been paying exorbitant fees to hire the SCG to stage Test matches, and had also used the Sydney Sports Ground next to it for other major representative fixtures. This meant that rugby authorities not only had to foot the bill for ground hire, but also to abide by the sponsorship, brewery, and food-licensing deals that those grounds had already secured. All this imposed limitations on how much revenue rugby authorities could generate from their highest-profile matches. So it was an appealing prospect to have a rugby headquarters in Sydney, akin to the Ballymore ground in Brisbane, where the game could reap the full commercial benefits of its showcase matches.

It was primarily for this reason that back in the mid-1980s, when plans for the expansion of Concord Oval were first unveiled, enthusiasm for the vision was unbridled.

Nick Farr-Jones called it 'the beginning of a great new era for Rugby Union', with the ground bound to become 'our own exclusive territory ... where Sydney, New South Wales, and Australian teams will take on all comers'. One of the ground's developers said it would be a 'world-class showpiece for Australian rugby' to rival Auckland's Eden Park, providing 'benefits hitherto unknown in Australia'. Unlike the SCG, fans would get 'an unmatched view' of the game with grandstands that 'closely surround the action'. As full-page advertisements in all the major newspapers announced, 'Twickenham, Cardiff Arms Park, Ballymore, and now, at long last ...'

But the plans were never realised. The dream of a 40,000-seat stadium died, and by 1989, after only two seasons, rugby Test matches moved back to Moore Park and the new Sydney Football Stadium, which had been finished in time for the Australian bicentenary. Later, they moved again to Homebush and the arena built for the 2000 Olympics. That in itself brought another round of huffing and puffing from rugby types, bemoaning once more their enforced great trek to western Sydney. But Concord continued to host grand finals of the Sydney rugby competition and occasional matches by the Waratahs against visiting touring sides. Its mostly empty stands even on those occasions were a perpetual reminder of the faded dream.

It speaks volumes for the current state of rugby in Australia that Concord's memory can be so transformed that it has now become, for some players at least, a source of fond reverie. By 2020, Campese had changed his mind about where the ground sat in his pantheon of reminiscences. At dusk one evening during the demolition, when the workers had gone home and the bulldozers sat silent, Campese paid a solitary, reflective visit to witness the scene. He said that as he walked around the ground, the memories of his career 'came flooding back to me'. He wanted to see Concord to 'take in those memories for the last time'.[3]

The memory that holds the most cherished place for Campese is the 1987 World Cup semi-final against France on 13 June. During that game, he broke the world try-scoring record (held by the Scotsman Ian Smith) by notching his twenty-fifth. The match had a dramatic ebb and flow in the scoreline, and is now widely remembered as one of the most exciting matches in rugby history. As *Midi Olympique*'s Jacques Verdier wrote at the time, it was a '*grande symphonie ... un grand morceau de rugby en plusieurs actes*', ('a grand symphony ... a rugby composition in multiple acts'), and the day that the French XV '*est entré dans la legende*' ('became legendary') when it beat Australia by 30–24.

Campese's try was overshadowed by the desperate, surging lunge for the corner by French fullback Serge Blanco in the dying minutes of the match to sink Australia. *L'Equipe*'s Denis Lalanne called that score an '*essai de chien, essai de reve et de tous les saints, essai gros comme le Pacifique*' ('a dog of a try, and yet the try of dreams and all the saints, a try as big as the Pacific Ocean').[4] As the whistle blew, French spectators sang the Marseillaise and waved the tricolour vigorously across the length and breadth of the grandstands.

Some of the greatest legends in the history of the French game — Pierre Berbizier, Eric Champ, Dominique Erbani, Philippe Sella, Denis Charvet, and Laurent Rodriguez — embraced as the weight of their win started to sink in. The Australian team, which had been considered favourites for the tournament, were on their knees, vanquished and dejected.

At Concord, too, Campese had played in six winning grand finals for the Randwick rugby club, represented New South Wales against Wales, England, and countless New Zealand provincial sides, and turned out for the Australian sevens team in a famous win over their New Zealand opponents. All this was on Campese's mind. He wanted to be there, too, he told the author, for the 'priceless memories' that the venue held for those 'who came before and after me'.

But what shocked Campese that evening — what saddened him intensely — was that the two enormous, iconic photographs of Australian rugby history, which had been on the walls above the entrance to the dressing rooms underneath the main grandstand, had been pulled down, broken up into pieces, and strewn across the floor, to be swept away as debris. As Campese said, 'We just seem to throw it away ... it's very scary, and very sad.' Those photos were of the 1927–28 Waratahs — often ennobled as the side that had first symbolised a particularly Australian style of 'running rugby'. That team contained the famous centre Cyril Towers, described as the father of the 'running game', the approach mastered by the Randwick and Australian sides of the 1980s. The other was of legendary Australian fullback Jim Lenehan, a pillar of the Wallaby backlines in the late 1950s and early 1960s. It was a photo of Lenehan at full stretch, about to score a try against South Africa at the SCG in 1965, with an enthralled ball boy on the sideline, mouth agape, clearly revelling in the moment.

As Campese concluded in a social media post: 'Almost 100 years of history gone. What has happened to us?'

Many Australian rugby supporters today are asking the same question, albeit not about the demise of Concord Oval. They are asking what happened to Wallaby success and to the style of rugby associated with that era. It is precisely this acute sense of loss — driven by the assumptions that professional rugby will no more allow for the cheeky and unpredictable talents of a Campese — that underlines why this particular Australian player still speaks to these times. So heavily scripted and over-regulated has the game of rugby become that the liberating style that Campese brought to a match — an athlete cutting loose when he took to the field, the impossible becoming somehow possible, the unthinkable somehow doable — appears consigned now to a short burst of archival memory, trapped within the three-minute clips of his tries that can be summoned up on YouTube.

If Campese stood at a 'slight angle to the universe', then arguably that angle has been straightened by incessant drills and routines, ironed out by the relentless focus on method, flattened by the obsession with patterns of play. Rugby has become more rigid, more structured, and subject to greater strictures by coaches, administrators, and lawmakers. The idea of a player such as Campese coming along and simply saying that his philosophy is to 'take one's chances' is now barely conceivable. No wonder one British rugby writer, Mick Cleary, once hailed Campese as a 'glorious, wild exception to the current vogue for corporate effort'.[5]

Rugby in Australia presents both an affirmation and inversion of Barry Humphries' celebrated quip about the country itself — that it was 'endlessly coming of age'. As this book has shown, moments of on-field triumph in 1980, 1984, 1986, and 1991 have brought forth the conclusion that the sport had finally gained its identity at home and respect abroad. But it has been constantly dying, too. At moments of decline, the prophets of doom are never far away. Campese was one of them. Five years before he stopped playing for the Wallabies, Campese was already pronouncing rugby to be a 'dying sport' — in the process of being engulfed by the publicity machine of Rugby League. As a result of what he perceived as a slip in basic skills and teamwork, a lack of characters and personalities, and overly cautious coaching, Campese saw a grim future.

Just over a decade later, as the game continued to navigate the early stages of the professional era, he was virtually giving the sport its burial rites, lamenting a game that had become 'robotic and static', haunted by 'negative attitudes', beset by 'buzzwords' and coaching philosophies that blunted 'the creativity of players'. That capacity for 'high risk', he noted, 'had been pulled back': he could have been talking about the man from Snowy River opting not to plunge headlong over that mountainside. 'The good old days had definitely gone,' Campese bemoaned, 'so I might as well go with them.'[6]

But those 'good old days' were profoundly different from the game in the professional era. For one thing, the number of tackles increased dramatically: statistical analysis of Test matches has revealed that whereas in the 1980s and 1990s there was an average of 100 tackles per match, today that number is closer to 300. To watch a match from the amateur era now, argues Michael Aylwin, is to be 'astonished at the way the game once was ... there is a glaring lack of discernible defensive systems, certainly ones of any urgency'.[7] Now, however, the players have been turned into self-guided projectiles, with all the ramifications that the impact of tackles has had for injuries and especially concussion.

No statistic, of course, will long fog the rosy-coloured lens of hindsight. As Denis Lalanne put it in a different context, those who 'have left an adventure behind them can no longer share the feelings of the adventurers'. A 'sort of disharmony between past and present that you can do nothing about insinuates itself slowly, like rust, between the consciousness of the "old soldiers" and the living virtues of the new recruits'.[8] Or, as cricket writer Neville Cardus said on one occasion, 'The Present is usually impatient when the glories of the Past are dinned in its ears.'[9]

Curiously enough, the golden period of Australian rugby might well have sown the seeds of the game's later troubles. The sense of entitlement to that kind of achievement, particularly among some of the game's administrators, is surely part of the reason why complacency and maladministration have plagued the sport since the late 1990s. The uninformed rugby buff in Australia, writes Dick Marks, came to believe that the Wallabies were owed this kind of success.[10] Yet that period from 1979 to 1999, from the year Australia won its first Bledisloe Cup in three decades to the second World Cup triumph in Cardiff, might instead be seen as something of an aberration, a period in which the right combination of coaches — among them, Marks himself, Brian O'Shea, Alec Evans, Bob Dwyer, and Alan Jones, guided an extraordinarily talented group of players to a series of memorable triumphs.

As Aylwin notes, for a 'modestly sized nation to boast double world champions in their fourth code of football is some achievement'.[11] Taking the long view, Australian rugby's record until the mid-1970s, with the exception of some stirring victories here and there, had been rather dim. The double irony is that the winning record of the 1980s and 1990s, and Campese's brilliance in particular, put the game on such a footing that it virtually had to go professional. Once it did, the limitations of its reach were cruelly exposed in the most saturated winter football market in the world. Aylwin is right to point out that Australian rugby's 'travails since 2003 [therefore] fit more snugly into the narrative of the first 100 years than the golden 20 at the turn of the century'.[12]

Campese felt the end of this era as keenly as his former teammates did. But perhaps he felt it even more, since he had no ready-made professional career to fall back into once the final whistle blew. Campese spoke often of his fear of having to come to terms with the end of his rugby career. He would 'experience a void', he thought, 'which I wonder if I shall ever manage to fill'.[13] As Gideon Haigh has noted, athletes typically experience death twice: 'the first time with the end of their competitive span'.[14] Campese soon filled that void with marriage, family, and a host of rugby-related duties, running his sports stores in Sydney, undertaking public speaking, and engaging in coaching clinics. To this day, he retains a feeling that the game still won't accept him, and still feels the barbs and criticisms from his playing days — especially those related to the Lions series of 1989. He would not be the first sportsperson to struggle to come to terms with the drop from the heights of stardom to the humdrum of everyday life, to not being as widely recognised anymore. With that has come a seemingly constant need for validation of his legacy to the game.

Campese has also found himself, on occasion, falling foul of a changing public culture, where his off-hand, impulsive comments, once a staple of his relationship with the media, have rebounded on him, revealing attitudes out of touch with twenty-first-century standards and expectations. He created a furore in 2012 when, on Twitter, he criticised the appointment of Georgina Robinson as rugby correspondent for the *Sydney Morning Herald*. Why did the *Herald*, he asked, 'get a girl to write about rugby?' The tweet was subsequently deleted, but the damage had been done, with Campese roundly condemned for the comments by then current Wallaby David Pocock and a raft of former players.

The following year, he again took to Twitter to express his agreement with comments made by ex-cricketer Doug Walters to the effect that Pakistan-born spin bowler Fawad Ahmed should not be selected to play for Australia if he refused to wear a beer sponsor's logo on the team uniform. Ahmed, who had left Pakistan in 2009 as a refugee, had told cricket authorities that he was not comfortable wearing a Victoria Bitter logo on his shirt due to his Islamic beliefs. He had 'probably come to Australia for a better life', Campese added, but was 'now telling people what he wants'. Yet Walters was the epitome of the beer-swilling cricket culture of the 1970s, the very culture that Campese had abhorred in rugby. This unsavoury episode showed once more the gap between what is deemed acceptable in a contemporary multicultural society and what is instantly recognised as a view harking back to a lost past.

~

What remains is the question of how, ultimately, Campese's impact on the sport in Australia, and indeed worldwide, is to be properly assessed. The point here is surely to see Campese as much on his own terms as it is to recognise that he was part of a Wallaby team that brought a thrilling style of play to that era, a style that had the editors of *Midi Olympique* in 1991 hailing it as '*le rugby de demain*', 'the rugby of tomorrow'. Those teams of the 1980s and 1990s do have their own zeitgeist, a group of players who thought and played in a certain way.[15] As Mark Ella put it, this was a 'different style of football altogether ... we just didn't want to waste possession' of the ball.[16]

Putting aside the tallies alongside his name — the once world record number of tries and the centenary of Tests that he played in — the question is whether Campese belongs in a different category of rugby player by virtue of his unique skills. To reach any kind of reasonable conclusion here, the mystical qualities attached to him by journalists, and indeed by Campese himself, need to be disentangled from his actual abilities as an athlete, and his tireless dedication to practice and perfection, as well as the effect he had on those watching him.

Campese often gave an off-hand excuse for his brilliance, saying that he simply did not know which way his legs were taking him. Alan Jones agreed, pointing out that Campese 'couldn't define what he did', while South African rugby correspondent Dean Viljoen could, on the one hand, praise the 'sheer artistry and chutzpah of an extraordinarily gifted player', and yet confess to being 'still totally in the dark about what motivates the man'.[17] It is, of course, impossible to know what was going on in Campese's head the moment he took the ball, especially when he continues to state that he was there, above all, to enjoy himself. And a key ingredient of that enjoyment was his near-complete lack of inhibition — a quality noted from the very beginning of his career. Campese's teammates in Queanbeyan said they had never seen such confidence in a seventeen-year-old, such willingness to try anything — from anywhere. That makes Bob Dwyer's observation of Campese probably closest to peeling the mask away from the mystery: Campese 'will never die not knowing the limits of his rugby abilities'.[18]

There can be no doubting, however, that in the time his reputation was made, it was Campese's sheer speed that caught the eye. Campese never claimed lightning pace over 100 metres, but his speed over the first five to ten metres was nothing short of electrifying. As Phillip Derriman wrote in 1983, 'his speed looks exceptional from the sideline'; '[a] moment is all he needs to go through the gate'.[19] Or, as Wanda Jamrozik put it: 'Campese in flight paralyses opposing players, astonishes spectators, appears capable of stretching and bending time itself.'[20] Powers of acceleration, though, are one thing: doing so while swerving and sidestepping is quite another. This was why Jamrozik proposed that Campese reached a 'state of grace' on the field — that silent yet scintillating ghosting through gaps that appeared to set him apart from so many of his contemporaries. What the former English fly-half Jonny Wilkinson said recently of All Black fly-half Dan Carter is equally applicable, if not more so, to David Campese: he 'had an influence on the game far greater than [his] own space'.[21]

That quality, as in the case of Carter and others, came from an ability to anticipate what was about to unfold — in other words, the capacity to read the game, to discern the underlying patterns of play, where others saw only disconnected shards. It is a quality that military strategists and foreign-policy planners crave: the gift of seeing around corners. The quality is not something that can be coached, affirmed the former Welsh and British Lions centre John

Dawes: it is 'innate'.[22] Coaches, said Carwyn James, could only take players to 'the conscious level', whereas knowing where the flow of the game is headed lies in the realm of the subconscious.[23] It was perhaps for this reason that Campese reflected on his desire to play the game 'above the level of the sublime'.[24] Spiro Zavos claimed that Campese had an ability to 'see things in slow motion'.[25] And Campese himself once told Evan Whitton that 'I never go where the ball is; I go where it is going.'[26]

Here, the notion of a category difference for Campese is probably less secure, since those around him in this era — especially Mark Ella, but also Michael Lynagh and Nick Farr-Jones — were all players who possessed the same kind of anticipatory quality. Campese's near-telepathic link with Ella has been discussed, yet it ought not be forgotten that his combination with Farr-Jones led to many of the tries he scored at the provincial and international level.

But, in this period at least, Campese was surely unsurpassed in the effect he had on spectators both in Australia and overseas. He brought new people to the sport: people came to watch Campese play. He believed there was a solemn pact between player and spectator — the latter had paid to be entertained, and it was his responsibility to provide it, even at the cost of breaching convention, and of losing winnable games. But what CLR James said of Victor Trumper is also applicable to Campese: he 'so reshaped the medium that it gave new satisfactions to new people'.[27] Well might many have sneered at Campese's mistakes, but the very same people hardly kept away; they couldn't avert their eyes the moment the ball came his way, or the moments he popped up randomly in the play to find the ball for himself. Peter FitzSimons aptly described the 'electric current that ran under every seat in the grandstand', pulsing every time Campese took the ball.

The ancient Greek writer and rhetorician Lucian could have been describing any stadium in which Campese was playing when he wrote to explain why the Greeks were so preoccupied with their games. He talked of:

> [The] idea of pleasure that you would have if you were seated in the middle of anxious spectators, watching the courage of the athletes, the beauty of their bodies, their splendid poses, their extraordinary suppleness, their tireless energy, their unconquerable courage, their unceasing efforts to win a victory. I am sure you would not cease to overwhelm them with praise, to shout again and again, to applaud.

The charge that Campese lacked courage will not stand up to scrutiny — one need only watch his running of the ball straight into the briar bush of the Irish forward pack in that jolting quarter-final in 1991 — and it was his ability to keep hold of the ball on that occasion which guaranteed the Australian side possession at the scrum from which they scored the winning try. Or take his running straight through the middle of virtually the entire All Black forward pack during the first Test in Sydney in the 1992 series, a move from which he almost scored.

The flipside of this natural talent was his dedication to training and to keeping himself fresh. As Mark Ella says, 'What Campese did produce wasn't by accident ... he just got better as he got older'.[28] That judgement was reinforced by former All Black coach John Hart, who remarked that what stood Campese apart from the rest was his constantly innovative approach to the game — he was, Hart said, as different and intriguing later in his career as he was when he first stepped onto the world rugby scene.[29] Referring to what he called Campese's 'utter professionalism', Alan Jones said that 'we got it from him every time'. Stu Wilson, the first player that Campese came up against in a rugby international, gave the most complete expression to this capacity for constant reinvention, from a player who became an ever-moving target:

Normally, after one year, a guy who's got a gift like Campese's got — and it is a gift — you work him out. But no matter how many times we tried to put the screws on Campese or close up the shop on him, he had an unbelievable ability to do something completely unexpected, something which was quite frightening but would also make us want to applaud the brilliance of a great player ... What he can do is beat guys like a whiff of air; he just glides through gaps. No matter how hard you concentrate — I mean, the All Blacks' backline used to say over and over 'We've got to keep Campo closed down all day' — you relax for just one second when you think no-one in their right mind would try to run the ball from there, and that's just when it happens. That's when he does it. The thing that sets Campese apart from the other players is that he's relaxed. The more relaxed he is, the better he plays. If you see Campo a bit wound up at the start of the game, he's not the same player. When he's nice and relaxed, when he's chatting to the ref and the touch judges, when he's winking at the ball-boys, that's when he's dangerous.[30]

I return to where this book began — to those early moments when Campese's talent was first discovered by the people who would influence the path he would ultimately take in the game. In 1982, at an Australian Under-21 trial match played at the Randwick Army Barracks in Sydney, a group of selectors, including Brian O'Shea and former Wallaby Arthur McGill, gathered to assess that year's crop of hopefuls. O'Shea was a former prop forward in the Newcastle rugby competition, and, naturally enough, had been tasked that day with watching the forwards. He had been the coach of the victorious Newcastle University premiership side of 1966, and went on not only to coach New South Wales but to play a senior leadership role in the rugby program at the Australian Institute of Sport and in preparing the Wallabies' 1991 World Cup side.

O'Shea vividly recalls that at half-time, Arthur McGill, who had played fullback for Australia in twenty-one Tests from 1968 to 1973, came rushing up to break the news to the other selectors about what he'd just witnessed. McGill was breathless, in a state of high excitement and barely able to speak. When the words did come, he simply said, 'You have to see this skinny little kid.' He was talking about David Campese.

McGill was apparently prone to these flights of oratorical fancy, given to waxing lyrical about the next big thing. But this time, it seemed different. This time, there was something in his voice, in his very agitation, that conveyed the exhilaration of discovery. So, during the second half of the match, all the selectors trained their eyes on the young fullback from Queanbeyan. They were agreed. This player was clearly destined for national honours, although they were worried that his slight frame might not withstand the rigours of Test rugby. Yet they were captivated by the young Campese's propensity to turn up at all points of the pitch. To paraphrase Seamus Heaney, he was already 'filling the element with signatures on his own frequency'.[31]

'He touched the ball so many times,' O'Shea remembers. 'He was just everywhere the ball was.'[32]

ACKNOWLEDGEMENTS

So many have helped, advised, and supported me in the writing of this book. First, my thanks go to David Campese himself, who, from the moment he was approached about the idea, never hesitated to help in any way he could — with countless in-person interviews and conversations, and by providing access to his personal collection of newspaper articles, magazines, and photographs. David also facilitated contact with his vast network across the rugby world, but at no stage did he attempt to influence the direction I wanted to take or the content of the work. David was unfailing in responding to my many requests for information.

From the start, too, I was fortunate to have the friendship, encouragement, and unstinting support of Elena Collinson, who read and commented on scratchy early drafts and book proposals, and who never once expressed bemusement at a political and foreign policy historian suddenly taking up his pen to write about rugby. Her enthusiasm for this project sustained my determination to keep going with it.

To my publisher, Henry Rosenbloom, I owe a special thanks. Henry engaged with the work in every respect, and his elegant editorial interventions improved this book. Thanks must go, too, to Julian Welch, by far the best proofreader I have worked with, and also to Bella Li and Mick Pilkington at Scribe, who worked tirelessly in shepherding this book through the production phase. Greg Harris, Gideon Haigh, Spiro Zavos, Blaise Dufal, and Gordon Bray, in critical conversations at the start of the process and throughout, not only helped to shape the early thinking for the work, but also instilled in me confidence that it could be done. My friend Max Suich read draft chapters and made incisive comments and suggestions that improved the work. My research assistant, Daniel Seaton, was simply brilliant, and this book also benefited from conversations with him about the nature of sport, art, and genius. His is a name to watch out for, not only in the writing of Australian history, but also in the chronicling of cricket.

Former Wallaby coaches Bob Dwyer and Alan Jones kindly spoke to me at length about Campese and the game of rugby. Bob Dwyer also generously agreed to write the foreword for the book. I got lost in the magical works of *L'Equipe*'s Denis Lalanne, perhaps the greatest ever writer on the game. Others who spoke to me about Campese included Malcolm Knox, Ben Ball, James Payten, Iain Payten, Mark Ella, Roger Gould, Bob Egerton, Nick Farr-Jones, Vittorio Munari, Andrew Clark, Hugh Summerhayes, and Peter J Boyle.

In Queanbeyan, Melanie Debenham provided access to her records of the Queanbeyan Whites, including some of the photos that feature in this book, while former Whites players Graeme Hughes, Phil Hawke, and Peter Stumbles painted their vivid pictures of a young Campese. I am grateful, too, to the librarians of the Mitchell Library for their assistance in accessing the Campese papers held at that institution. My parents, Jeannie Addison and Bernie Curran, also read and commented on draft chapters. To my daughters, Pia and Ella, you are entirely forgiven for the occasional eye roll at your dad's decision to take on the writing of this book. But your love has also sustained me, as it always will.

NOTES

Introduction: Off the Edge

1   Richard White, 'The Man from Snowy River', *The Australian*, 17 October 1995.

2   Many in the crowd that day swore he was offside, but the try stood. *Rothmans Australian Rugby Yearbook*, 1982.

3   Official Match Programme, *New Zealand v Australia*, Lancaster Park, Christchurch, 14 August 1982, author's collection.

4   Alex Wilson, 'Sparkling Campese sets the pace', *Rugby World* (January 1984).

5   *The Sydney Morning Herald* (hereafter *SMH*), 24 October 1996.

6   Gideon Haigh, *Stroke of Genius: Victor Trumper and the shot that changed cricket*, p. 255.

7   Loane, quoted in Cockerill, 'Campese: shy and mighty', *Inside Sport* (1993), p. 30.

8   The poem can be read here: //www.nancyesims.com/winners-are-people-like-you.html.

9   Wanda Jamrozik, 'Campese and me', *The Independent Monthly* (1996).

10 'Campese, le marchand de rêves', *Sud-Ouest*, 20 October 1993, in

David Campese papers, Mitchell Library, Box 4.

11 Conversation with Malcolm Knox, 22 February 2021.

12 Spiro Zavos, *SMH*, 22 August 1995; for Muhammad Ali comparison, see quote by Grant Batty, a former All Black, in *The Canberra Times*, 2 September 1982; Mark Abernathy in *Inside Sport* described Campese as having a 'Jackson Pollock type flair', while British rugby writer Frank Keating compared Keating to Nijinsky; 'Mona Lisa' smile is quoted by Bruce Wilson in *The Courier-Mail*, 2 November 1991.

13 Quoted in 'Campese — the name they say in heaven', *The Sun-Herald*, 12 June 1994.

14 Stephen Jones, 'Campo, Campo, Campionissimo', *The Sunday Times* (UK), 3 November 1991.

15 Stephen Jones (ed.), *Rothmans Rugby Union Yearbook 1992–93* (London: Headline Book Publishing, 1993), p. 12.

16 Jamrozik, 'David Campese and me'.

17 Philip Derriman, 'Goosestep a simple but deadly trick', *SMH*, 12 May 1985.

18 Teresa Lacerda and Stephen Mumford, 'The Genius in Art and Sport: a contribution to the investigation of aesthetics of sport', *Journal of the Philosophy of Sport*, no. 37 (2010), pp. 185, 189.

19 Johan Cruyff, *My Turn* (London: Pan Macmillan, 2016), p. 56.

20 Evan Whitton, 'The zap! zap! zap! of David Campese', originally published in *The National Times*, in Godfrey Smith (ed.), *Take the Ball and Run: a rugby anthology* (London: Pavillion, 1991), p. 63.

21 Batty, quoted in *The Canberra Times*, 2 September 1982.

22 Sean Smith, *The Union Game: a rugby history* (London: BBC Books, 1999), p. 254.

23 Bill McLaren, *Rugby's Great Heroes and Entertainers* (London: Hodder & Stoughton, 2003), p. 186.

24 Prime Minister Paul Keating, Transcript of interview with Angela Caterns, JJJ, 15 December 1995, transcript, www.pmtranscripts. pmc.gov.au, accessed 4 February 2020.

25 Campese, quoted in *The Sun-Herald*, 12 June 1994.

26 Campese, quoted in *The Daily Telegraph-Mirror*, 25 June 1994.

27 Seamus Heaney, in Denis O'Driscoll, *Stepping Stones: interviews with Seamus Heaney*, p. 346.

Chapter One: Movement

1 David Campese with Peter Bills, *On a Wing and a Prayer: the autobiography of David Campese*, pp. 112–13.

2 Mark Ella, *Running Rugby* (Sydney: ABC Books, 1995), p. 20.

3 Bret Harris, *Michael O'Connor: the best of both worlds* (Sydney: Pan Macmillan, 1991), p. 64.

4 Interview with Roger Gould, 10 December 2020.

5 Harris, *Michael O'Connor*, p. 51.

6 On the new nationalism, see James Curran and Stuart Ward, *The Unknown Nation: Australia after Empire* (Carlton: Melbourne University Press, 2010).

7 Interview from *Rugby in the 70s*, ABC TV documentary, 2006.

8 Don Cameron, *Rugby Triumphant: the All Blacks in Australia and Wales* (Auckland: Hodder & Stoughton, 1981), pp. 106–7.

9 See Harris, *Michael O'Connor*, p. 55; *Australia v New Zealand*, Third Test Match Program, Sydney, 12 July 1980, author's collection.

10 Tony Shaw, quoted in Philip Derriman, *The Rise and Rise of Australian Rugby* (Sydney: ABC Books, 2001), p. 71.

11 *The Sun-Herald*, 13 July 1980.

12 The replay can be found on YouTube at www.youtube.com/watch?v=SOE-tAL50B4.

13 Bret Harris, *Ella, Ella, Ella* (Sydney: Little Hills Press, 1984), p. 76.

14 Tony Shaw, quoted in Derriman, *The Rise and Rise of Australian Rugby*, p. 68.

15 Evan Whitton, 'Australians have much to thank England for', in *England v Australia*, Match Program, 3 November 1984, Twickenham, p. 43, author's collection.

16 Carwyn James, quoted in Alun Gibbard, *Into the Wind: the life of*

Carwyn James (Ceredigion: Y Lolfa, 2017), p. 195.

17 Ella, *Running Rugby*, pp. 12–14, 17.

18 Ibid., p. 26.

19 Michael Foster, 'Exhilarating and exciting rugby', *The Canberra Times*, 13 July 1980.

20 Greg Cornelsen, quoted in Derriman, *The Rise and Rise of Australian Rugby*, p. 70.

21 Ella, *Running Rugby*, p. 25.

22 Cameron, *Rugby Triumphant*, p. 128.

23 *The Sun-Herald*, 13 July 1980; *SMH*, 14 July 1980.

24 See *The Courier-Mail, The Sun-Herald*, and *The Australian*, 13 July 1980.

25 See *The Australian* and *The Sun-Herald*, 13 July 1980.

26 *The Sun-Herald*, 13 July 1980.

Chapter Two: Freedom

1 Campese, *Still Entertaining* (Sydney: Flick Pass Productions, 2003), pp. 16–17.

2 Duncan Hamilton, *The Great Romantic: cricket and the golden age of Neville Cardus* (London: Hodder & Stoughton, 2019), pp. 217, 220.

3 Campese, *Still Entertaining*, p. 16.

4 Ibid., p. 17.

5 See Dwight Zakus and Peter Horton, 'A Professional Game for Gentlemen: Rugby Union's transformation', in Bob Stewart (ed.), *The Games Are Not the Same: the political economy of football in Australia* (Carlton: Melbourne University Press, 2007), p. 147.

6 Ian Cockerill, *Inside Sport.*

7 SMW Withycombe, *Town in Transition: a socio-economic history of Queanbeyan, New South Wales, 1945–85* (Canberra: Canberra Publishing and Printing, n.d.), p. 164.

8 Bob Hitchcock, interview, Campese, *Rugby's My Life* DVD.

9 Campese, *On a Wing and a Prayer*, p. 23.

10 David Campese, in David Campese and Mal Meninga, *My Game, Your Game: David Campese and Mal Meninga talk football* (Sydney: Pan Macmillan, 1996), p. 180.

11 Campese, *Still Entertaining*, p. 128; Campese, *On a Wing and a Prayer*, pp. 14–15.

12 Campese, *On a Wing and a Prayer*, p. 15.

13 Campese, conversation with the author, 23 October 2010.

14 *The Queanbeyan Age* (hereafter '*QA*'), 23 July 1982.

15 *QA*, 2 May 1972.

16 Email from Melanie Debenham to author, 1 October 2020.

17 Interview with Peter Stumbles, Phil Hawke, and Graham Hughes, 22 September 2020.

18 Jack Pollard, *Australian Rugby: the game and the players* (Sydney: Pan Macmillan, 1994, p. 20.

19 Thierry Teret, 'Learning to be a Man: French rugby and masculinity', in TJL Chandler and J Nauright (eds), *Making the Rugby World: race, gender and commerce* (Frank Cass: London, 1999), pp. 63–87.

20 *QA*, 9 May 1980; See also Pollard, *Australian Rugby*, p. 164.

21 Campese and Meninga, *My Game, Your Game*, p. 185.

22 *QA*, 12 May 1980.

23 *QA*, 30 June 1980.

24 *QA*, 4 July 1980.

25 *QA*, 8 September 1980.

26 *QA*, 13 May 1981.

27 *QA*, 25 May 1981.

28 *QA*, 29 July 1981.

29 *QA*, 17 August 1981.

30 *QA*, 21 September 1981.

31 Withycombe, *Town in Transition*, p. x.

32 *QA*, 5 May 1982.

33 As heard on documentary *Rugby's My Life*.

34 *QA*, 14 July 1982.

35 *QA*, 28 May 1982.

36 Interview with Alan Jones, 28 August 2020.

37 Zavos, quoted in *Rugby's My Life* documentary.

38 *QA*, 23 July 1982.

39 *QA*, 12 July 1982, 8 September 1982, Bray, ABC TV commentary.

40 *The Canberra Times*, 1 August 1982.

41 *The Canberra Times*, 11 September 1982.

42 *QA*, 8 September 1982.

43 *The Canberra Times*, 2 September 1982.

44 Ella, *Running Rugby*, pp. 37–39.

45 Bret Harris and Mark Ella, *Ella: the definitive biography* (Sydney: Random House, 2007), p. 182; Interview with Mark Ella, 8 July 2021.

46 Ella, *Running Rugby*, p. 39.

47 Interview with Roger Gould, 10 December 2020.

48 Ella, *Running Rugby*, p. 40.

49 Harris and Ella, *Ella*, p. 182.

50 *The Canberra Times*, 9 April 1983.

51 *QA*, 22 February 1984.

52 Campese, *Still Entertaining*, p. 54.

53 Shelley, *In Defence of Poetry*.

Chapter Three: Acclaim

1 *The Sunday Times* (UK), 5 March 1989.

2 Alun Richards, *Carwyn: a personal memoir* (Cardiff: Parthian, 2015), p. 73.

3 McClaren's commentary can be heard here: www.youtube.com/watch?v=z3FPJbGB2xg.

4 Frank Keating, *The Guardian*, 2 November 1991; Stephen Jones, *The Sunday Times* (UK), 3 November 1991.

5 *The Australian*, 28 November 1988; *SMH*, 28 November 1988.

6 Davies, quoted in *The Sunday Times* (UK), 5 March 1989.

7 Owen Sheers, *Calon: a journey to the heart of Welsh rugby* (London: Faber & Faber, 2013), p. 24.

8 David Foster Wallace, 'Federer as Religious Experience', *The New York Times Magazine*, 20 August 2006; Lacerda and Mumford, p. 187.

9 Spiro Zavos, *How to Watch a Game of Rugby* (Wellington: AWA Press, 2004), pp. 81, 101, 103.

10 Carwyn James, quoted in Gibbard, *Into the Wind*, p. 300.

11 Mick Cleary, 'Campo: dishing it out sweet and sour', *Rugby World & Post* (June 1992), pp. 18–22.

12 Stephen Jones, *The Sunday Times* (UK), 30 November 1992.

13 Greg Growden, 'It's Campo and the tabloid magic', *SMH*, November 1992.

14 Interview with David Campese, 18 September 2020; see also David Campese, 'Mixed Feelings of the Maestro Wing', in Ian Robertston (ed.), *The Official Book of the Rugby World Cup 1991* (London: Random House, 1991), p. 152.

15 *Rothmans Rugby Union Yearbook 1992–93* (London: Headline Book Publishing, 1992), pp. 9–10.

16 Greg Growden, 'David Campese … The Wizard of Oz', *Rugby 92: Official ARFU Tour Guide* (Sydney: Federal Publishing Company, 1992), p. 79.

17 Graeme Davison, 'The Imaginary Grandstand', *Meanjin*, vol. 61, no. 2 (2002), p. 6.

18 Viv Jenkins, 'The Long and the Short of It', *Rugby World* (February 1976), p. 3.

19 *Rugby World* (November 1981).

20 Slack, quoted in Dudley Doust, 'From Ulster history to Munster mystery', newspaper article, Campese papers.

21 Campese, *On a Wing and a Prayer*, p. 78.

22 Alex Wilson, 'Sparkling Campese sets the pace', *Rugby World* (January 1984), pp. 18–19.

23 Barry Newcombe, 'Watch out for the Aussies' goose-stepper', newspaper files, Campese papers.

24 Gideon Haigh, *Silent Revolutions: writings on cricket history* (Melbourne: Black Inc, 2006), pp. 21–23; see also Richard Holt,

'Don Bradman: an Australian hero who was loved in England', *Wisden Cricket Almanack*, 25 February 2020.

25 Norman Mair, *The Scotsman*, 10 December 1984.

26 'Tommo', 'Britain's bunch of slackers', Campese papers.

27 David Frost, 'Wallabies short and to point', *Rugby's Times*, 23 November 1984.

28 Bill Beaumont, column, *Rugby World* (December 1984), p. 28.

29 Gerald Davies, 'British gallery seeks recovery of lost art', Campese papers.

30 Smith, *The Union Game*, p. 251.

31 Evan Whitton, 'Aussie Torquemadas seek to extirpate Rugby Heresy', Scotland v Australia Match Programme, 8 December 1984, author's collection.

32 On the 1982 Kangaroos tour of the UK, see Mark Flanagan, *The Invincibles: the inside story of the 1982 Kangaroos, the team that changed rugby forever* (Sussex: Pitch Publishing, 2019).

33 Eddie Butler, quoted in Philip Derriman, *The Rise and Rise of Australian Rugby*, pp. 124–26.

34 Quotes by Taylor and Mason are in Terry Smith and Mark Ella, *Path to Victory: Wallaby power in the 1980s* (Sydney: ABC Books, 1987), p. 128.

35 Bill McClaren, *Rugby's Great Heroes and Entertainers*, p. 157.

36 Stephen Jones, 'Like giants amid pygmies', in Campese papers.

37 Pollard, *Australian Rugby*, p. 672.

38 Campese, *On a Wing and a Prayer*, p. 88.

39 Ibid., pp. 84, 90, 188–89, 222.

40 Ibid., pp. 214–15.

41 McClaren, *Rugby's Great Heroes and Entertainers*, p. 186; for Ackford's comment, see *The Daily Telegraph*, 30 November 1992.

42 'BBC defends Campese role', 17 December 2003, http://news.bbc.co.uk/sport2/hi/tv_and_radio/sports_personality_2003/3326741.stm.

43 Campese, *On a Wing and a Prayer*, p. 87.

44 John Kennedy, 'Arrivederci Campese', in Wales v Australia Match Program, 1 December 1996, author's collection.

Chapter Four: Outcast

1 Campese, *On a Wing and a Prayer*, p. 118.
2 Interview with Bob Dwyer, 10 July 2020.
3 FitzSimons, *Nick Farr-Jones* (Sydney: Random House, 1993), p. 199.
4 Nick Cain, 'Sydney Showdown: Lions clinch it', *Rugby World & Post* (August 1989), p. 40.
5 Stephen Jones, Tom English, Nick Cain, and David Barnes, *Behind the Lions* (Edinburgh: Birlinn Press, 2012), p. 334.
6 *SMH*, 17 July 1989; *The Australian*, 17 July 1989; *The Sun-Herald*, 16 July 1989.
7 *The Sunday Telegraph*, 16 July 1989.
8 *The Sunday Mail*, 16 July 1989.
9 Interview with Nick Farr-Jones, 27 November 2020.
10 *SMH*, 18 July 1989.
11 Correspondence, Nick Farr-Jones to the sports editor, *SMH*, 19 July 1989.
12 Interview with Nick Farr-Jones, 27 November 2020.
13 *The Daily Telegraph*, 18 July 1989.
14 Andrew Slack, *Noddy: the authorised biography of Michael Lynagh* (Melbourne: Heinemann, 2014), p. 179.
15 Campese, *On a Wing and a Prayer*, pp. 92–106.
16 Interview with Nick Farr-Jones, 27 November 2020.
17 Christian Ryan, *Golden Boy: Kim Hughes and the bad old days of Australian cricket* (Sydney: Allen & Unwin, 2009), pp. 134–36.
18 *SMH*, 15 July 1989.
19 *The Weekend Australian*, 15 July 1989.
20 *SMH*, 15 July 1989.
21 *The Weekend Australian*, 15 July 1989.
22 Nick Cain, column, *Rugby World & Post* (August 1982), p. 14.

23 Eddie Butler, column, *Rugby World & Post* (August 1982), p. 11.

24 *The Daily Telegraph-Mirror*, 1 July 1989.

25 Comments in *Behind the Lions*, pp. 332–34.

26 *The Daily Telegraph*, 18 July 1989.

27 *The Daily Telegraph*, 17 July 1989.

28 *The Whitbread Rugby World '90* (Oxford: Lennard, 1989), p. 45.

29 Campese, *On a Wing and a Prayer*, p. 123.

Chapter Five: Magic

1   Campese, *On a Wing and a Prayer*, p. 216.

2   Bob Dwyer, *The Winning Way* (Auckland: Rugby Press, 1992), p. 122.

3   Andrew Slack, *The Australian*, 28 July 1991.

4   CLR James, *Beyond a Boundary* (London: Vintage Classics, 2019, first edition 1963), pp. 138–39.

5   Clem Thomas, 'Crusading Wallabies shatter the champions' in Ian Robertson (ed.), *The Official Book of the Rugby World Cup 1991* (Sydney: Random House, 1991), pp. 124–27.

6   *Midol Mag*, December 1991, Campese papers.

7   Louis MacNeice, 'The Closing Album: 1 — Dublin', in Michael Longley (ed.), *Louis MacNeice: Selected Poems* (London: Faber & Faber, 2001), pp. 47–48.

8   Jim Tucker, 'Kiwis know Campo', *The Sun*, undated, Campese papers.

9   Barry John, 'Campese: the diamond' in Robertson (ed.), *The Official Book of the Rugby World Cup 1991*, p. 157.

10 Simon Poidevin, quoted in Greg Growden (ed.), *The Wallabies' World Cup!* (Sydney: Text Publishing, 1991), p. 21.

11 Dwyer, *The Winning Way*, p. 142.

12 Ibid., p. 143.

13 Denis Lalanne, *La mêlée fantastique*, translated by E Boyd Wilson (Wellington: AH and AW Reed, 1962), p. 50.

14 Andrew Clark, note to author, 21 October 2020.

15 Jim Tucker, 'David slays Goliath', *The Sun*, 28 October 1991.

16 Seamus Heaney, 'Trout', in Seamus Heaney, *Death of a Naturalist* (London: Faber & Faber, 1966), p. 26.

17 Jacques Verdier, *Midol Mag*, December 1991, Campese papers.

18 Hignell and Kirk, along with Bill Calcraft, were calling the match on ITV.

19 Slack, *Noddy*, p. 226.

20 'All Blacks nailed to Southern Cross', *Rugby World & Post* (December 1991), p. 73.

21 *Midol Mag*, December 1991, Campese papers.

22 Louis MacNeice, 'The Closing Album, 1 — Dublin'.

23 *SMH*, 21 November 1991.

24 See *SMH*, 21 November 1991; *The Australian*, 21 November 1991.

25 *SMH*, 21 November 1991.

26 John Huxley, Introduction to Growden (ed.), *The Wallabies' World Cup!*, p. 7.

27 *SMH*, 4 November 1991.

28 *The Australian*, 21 November 1991.

Chapter Six: Maestro

1 Louis MacNeice, 'Sports Pages', in MacNeice, *Selected Poems*, p. 155.

2 Frank Keating, reprinted in *SMH*, 23 October 1996.

3 Congratulatory telegrams on the occasion of 100th Test, Campese personal collection.

4 'Campese's century of Test matches', *The Australian*, 25 October 1996.

5 'Veteran genius still vital to our chances', *The Australian*, 26 May 1995.

6 Bruce Wilson, 'Bravo Campo', *The Daily Telegraph*, 25 October 1996.

7 Bob Dwyer, quoted in *The Daily Telegraph*, 18 July 1996.

8 Bruce Wilson, 'Why David's in a class of his own', *The Daily Telegraph*, 23 October 1996.

9   'Campo must get axe', *The Daily Telegraph*, undated, Campese personal collection.

10 Telegrams from R Mcgruther and J Breen, Campese personal collection, 21 October 1996.

11 *SMH*, 24 October 1996.

12 *The Australian*, 25 October 1996.

13 Ray Chesterton, 'Don't miss one last glimpse of bliss', *The Daily Telegraph*, 23 October 1996.

14 'There'll be no David, but we've got Goliath', *NZ Rugby News*, 19 July 1995.

15 Tony Collins, *The Oval World: a global history of Rugby* (London: Bloomsbury, 2015), p. 314.

16 Seamus Heaney, translation of Virgil's *Aeneid Book VI* (London: Faber & Faber, 2016), p. 3.

17 Collins, *The Oval World*, p. 314.

18 Gherardo Bonini, 'Rugby: the game for "real Italian men"', in JH Chandler and John Nauright (eds), *Making the Rugby World: race, gender and commerce* (London: Routledge, 1999), p. 101.

19 *Il Mondo del Rugby* (Gennaio, 1989), p. 4.

20 Chris Thau, 'Azzurri ... a case of the blues', *Rugby World & Post* (March 1989), pp. 40–41.

21 Carwyn James, quoted in Gibbard, *Into the Wind*, p. 334.

22 Richards, *Carwyn*, p. 9.

23 Interview with Roger Gould, 10 December 2020.

24 Carlo Gobbi, *La Gazetta dello Sport*, 3 June 1993.

25 Campese, *On a Wing and a Prayer*, pp. 44–48.

26 Interview with Vittorio Munari, 6 December 2020.

27 Undated Italian newspaper, likely early 1985, Campese personal collection.

28 Campese, postcard to his parents, Campese personal collection.

29 Lynagh, quoted in Slack, *Noddy*, p. 234.

30 Undated article, Carlo Gobbi, *La Gazetta dello Sport*, Campese personal collection.

31 Campese, *Still Entertaining*, p. 255 ff.

32 Campese, *On a Wing and a Prayer*, p. 50.

33 Campese, quoted in *La Gazetta dello Sport*, 3 June 1993.

34 *The Sunday Mail*, 1 September 1991.

35 'I, Campo', *The Daily Telegraph-Mirror*, 1 July 1992.

36 Pierre Lanfranchi and Alfred Wahl, 'The Immigrant as Hero: Kopa, Mekloufi and French football', *The International Journal of the History of Sport*, vol. 13, no. 1 (1996), pp. 114–27.

37 'Campese tempted by League dollars', *The Daily Mirror*, 1 May 1984.

38 Campese, *Still Entertaining*, p. 17.

39 Smith, *The Union Game*, p. 258.

40 Interview with Bob Dwyer, 10 July 2020.

41 *The Australian*, 7 October 1985; *The Canberra Times*, 6 October 1985.

42 Quotes from *The Australian*, 7 October 1985.

43 *SMH*, 8 October 1985.

44 *The Canberra Times*, 16 October 1985.

45 Philip Derriman, 'King Campo — simply the best', *SMH*, 27 February 1993.

46 Campese and Meninga, *My Game, Your Game*, p. 260.

47 Campese, *On a Wing and a Prayer*, p. 13.

48 The Winfield Cup was awarded to the winner of the New South Wales Rugby League Grand Final from 1982 to 1994, and then to the winner of the newly founded Australian Rugby League Grand Final in 1995.

49 See Campese, quoted in *SMH*, 27 February 1993; and Campese, *On a Wing and a Prayer*, pp. 198–99.

50 Mick Cleary, 'Licence to earn?', *Rugby World & Post* (March 1991), pp. 22–23.

51 Jim Tucker, 'Farr-Jones: time to go pro?', *Rugby World & Post* (August 1992), pp. 18–19.

52 Guy, quoted in Collins, *The Oval World*, pp. 471–72.

53 Campese, *Still Entertaining*, pp. 49–51.

54 Michael Aylwin with Mark Evans, *Unholy Union: when rugby collided with the modern world* (London: Constable, 2019), p. 8.

55 Mark Abernethy, 'The next incarnation of David Campese', *Inside Sport* (May, 1995) pp. 34–35.

56 Peter Jenkins, 'Campo — the maestro speaks', *Rugby 95* [magazine], pp. 39–40.

57 Mick Cleary, 'Death of the game', *Rugby World & Post* (August 1992), pp. 10–13.

58 Campese, *Still Entertaining*, p. 54.

59 Campese, quoted in *SMH*, 27 February 1993.

60 *The Daily Telegraph-Mirror*, 18 July 1995.

61 *The Daily Telegraph-Mirror*, 25 July 1995.

62 Spiro Zavos, 'Campo has the genius of Dally', *SMH*, 22 August 1995.

63 Spiro Zavos, 'Fragile talent on display — and gone', *SMH*, 5 March 1996.

64 Kennedy, 'Arrivederci Campese', author's collection.

65 *The Daily Telegraph-Mirror*, 3 and 10 December 1996.

66 Bruce Wilson, *The Daily Telegraph-Mirror*, 3 December 1996.

Conclusion: Amid the Rubble

1 Greg Growden, 'A grand vision 110 years in the making', in Norman Tasker (ed.), *Rugby 86: Official Publication of the NSW Rugby Union*, pp. 8–9.

2 Campese, *On a Wing and a Prayer*, pp. 111–12.

3 James Curran, 'L'Adieu a Concord Oval', *Midi-Olympique Mag* (September/October, 2020), pp. 50–55.

4 Lalanne quoted in Jacques Verdier, *Chroniques Ovales* (*Vingt ans de carnets de bord*) (Toulouse: Midi-Olympique editions, 2006), pp. 61–62.

5 Cleary, 'Campo', p. 20.

6 Campese, *On a Wing and a Prayer*, pp. 23–24; and *Still Entertaining*, pp. 6, 18–19, 86–87, 116.

7   Aylwin, *Unholy Union*, pp. 252, 257.

8   Lalanne, *La mêlée fantastique* p. 90.

9   Cardus, quoted in Duncan Hamilton, *The Great Romantic*, p. xix.

10 RJP Marks, *The Descent of Australian Rugby: hellish times for the game they play in heaven* (privately published, 2020), p. 65.

11 Aylwin, *Unholy Union*, p. 56.

12 Ibid., p. 290.

13 Campese, *On a Wing and a Prayer*, p. 211.

14 Haigh, *Stroke of Genius*, p. 214.

15 James, *Beyond a Boundary*, p. 48.

16 Interview with Mark Ella, 8 July 2020.

17 Viljoen, undated newspaper cutting, scrapbook of Wallaby tour to South Africa, 1992, Campese papers, ML MSS 5875.

18 Dwyer, quoted in *The Daily Telegraph-Mirror*, 4 July 1972.

19 *SMH*, 12 May 1983.

20 Jamrozik, 'David Campese and me', pp. 44–45.

21 Jonny Wilkinson, quoted in *Dan Carter: perfect 10*, DVD, 2019.

22 John Dawes, in John Reason (ed.), *How We Beat the All Blacks: the 1971 Lions Speak* (London: Rugby Books, 1972), p. 119.

23 Carwyn James, in Reason (ed.), *How We Beat the All Blacks*, p. 156.

24 Interview with David Campese, 6 July 2020.

25 Interview with Spiro Zavos, 10 September 2020.

26 Evan Whitton, 'A case for Campese', newspaper cutting, 1996, Campese personal collection.

27 James, *Beyond a Boundary*, p. 294.

28 Interview with Mark Ella, 10 July 2020.

29 Hart's comments were made in a DVD on Campese's career, *Rugby's My Life*.

30 Stu Wilson, quoted in *SMH*, 27 February 1993.

31 Adapted from Seamus Heaney, 'Station Island: XII' in *Station Island* (London: Faber & Faber, 1984), p. 94.

32 Interview with Brian O'Shea, November 2020.

SELECT BIBLIOGRAPHY

Aylwin, Michael, with Mark Evans, *Unholy Union: when rugby collided with the modern world* (London: Constable Books, 2019)

Campese, David, with Peter Bills, *On a Wing and a Prayer* (London: McDonald Queen Anne Press, 1991)

Campese, David, with Peter Jenkins, *Still Entertaining* (Sydney: Flick Pass Productions, 2003)

Campese, David and Mal Meninga, *My Game Your Game: David Campese and Mal Meninga talk football* (Sydney: Pan Macmillan, 1994)

Clark, David (ed.), *David Campese* (Sydney: Pan Macmillan, 1996)

Collins, Tony, *The Oval World: a global history of rugby* (London: Bloomsbury, 2015)

Derriman, Philip, *The Rise and Rise of Australian Rugby* (Sydney: ABC Books, 2001)

Dwyer, Bob, *The Winning Way* (Auckland: Rugby Press Limited, 1992)

Ella, Mark, *Running Rugby* (Sydney: ABC Books, 1995)

Ella, Mark and Terry Smith, *Path to Victory: Wallaby power in the 1980s* (Sydney: ABC Books, 1987)

FitzSimons, Peter, *Nick Farr-Jones: the authorised biography* (Sydney: Random House, 1993)

——, *The Rugby War* (Sydney: Harper Collins, 1996)

Gibbard, Alun, *Into the Wind: the life of Carwyn James* (Ceredigion: Y Lolfa, 2017)

Growden, Greg (ed.), *The Wallabies' World Cup!* (Sydney: Text Publishing, 1991)

——, *Inside the Wallabies: the real story* (Sydney: Allen & Unwin, 2010)

Haigh, Gideon, *On Warne* (Melbourne: Penguin, 2012)

——, *Stroke of Genius: Victor Trumper and the shot that changed cricket* (Melbourne: Penguin, 2016)

Hamilton, Duncan, *The Great Romantic: cricket and the golden age of Neville Cardus* (London: Hodder & Stoughton, 2019)

Harris, Bret, *Ella, Ella, Ella* (Sydney: Little Hills Press, 1984)

——, *Michael O'Connor: the best of both worlds* (Sydney: Pan Macmillan, 1991)

Harris, Bret, and Mark Ella, *Ella: the definitive biography* (Sydney: Random House, 2007)

Heaney, Seamus, *Opened Ground: poems 1966–1996* (London: Faber & Faber, 1998)

James, CLR, *Beyond a Boundary* (London: Hutchinson, 1963)

Jenkins, Peter and Matthew Alvarez, *Wallaby Gold: 100 Years of Australian Test Rugby* (Sydney: Random House, 1999)

Lalanne, Denis, *The Great Fight of the French Fifteen* (Wellington: AH and AW Reed, 1960)

——, *La mêlée fantastique* (Wellington: AH and AW Reed, 1962)

MacNiece, Louis, *Selected Poems* (London: Faber & Faber, 1988)

McLaren, Bill, *Rugby's Great Heroes and Entertainers* (London: Hodder & Stoughton, 2003)

——, *The Voice of Rugby: my autobiography* (London: Bantam Press, 2004)

Moore, Richard, *Slaying the Badger: Lemond, Hinault and the greatest ever Tour de France* (London: Yellow Jersey Press, 2012)

O'Driscoll, Dennis, *Stepping Stones: interviews with Seamus Heaney* (London: Faber & Faber, 2008)

Poidevin, Simon, *For Love Not Money: the Simon Poidevin story* (Sydney: ABC Books, 1990)

Pollard, Jack, *Australian Rugby: the game and the players* (Sydney: Pan Macmillan, 1994)

Reason, John, *How We Beat the All Blacks: the 1971 Lions speak* (London: Rugby Books, 1972)

Richards, Alun, *Carwyn: a personal memoir* (Cardiff: Parthian, 2015)

Ryan, Christian, *Golden Boy: Kim Hughes and the bad old days of Australian cricket* (Sydney: Allen & Unwin, 2009)

Sheers, Owen, *Calon: a journey to the heart of Welsh rugby* (London: Faber & Faber, 2013)

Slack, Andrew, *Noddy: the authorised biography of Michael Lynagh* (Melbourne: Heinemann, 1995)

Smith, Sean, *The Union Game: a rugby history* (London: BBC Books, 1999)

Starmer-Smith, Nigel and Ian Robertson, *BBC Rugby Special* (London: BBC Books, 1987)

Verdier, Jacques, *Chroniques Ovales: vingt ans de carnets de bord* (Toulouse: Midi Olympiques Editions, 2006)

Zavos, Spiro, *The Gold and the Black: the rugby battles for the Bledisloe Cup* (Sydney: Allen & Unwin, 1995)

——, *How to Watch a Game of Rugby* (Wellington: AWA Press, 2004)